PRAYERS THAT PREVAIL

The Believer's Manual of Prayers

By

Clift Richards & Lloyd Hildebrand

Victory House, Inc.
Tulsa, Oklahoma

PRAYERS THAT PREVAIL
Copyright © 1990 by K & C International, Inc.
ISBN 0-932081-25-8
All rights reserved
Printed in the United States of America

Published by Victory House, Inc.
P. O. Box 700238
Tulsa, OK 74170

Special purpose marketing by Gateway International, Inc.,
P. O. Box 702008, Tulsa, OK 74170.

TABLE OF CONTENTS

Acknowledgments

We wish to thank Lloyd Hildebrand, Clift Richards, and others who spent the many hours of research and writing needed to enable us to share the prayers and teaching in this book. Truly God's hand was upon them as they wrote.

— The Publisher

Books By
Clift Richards & Lloyd Hildebrand

PRAYERS THAT PREVAIL
(The Believer's Manual of Prayers)

PRAYERS THAT PREVAIL FOR AMERICA
(Changing a Nation Through Prayer)

CALL TO PRAYER

There is power in prayer and there is power in the Word of God. Combine these two dynamic sources with the power of the Holy Spirit, and explosive spiritual energy is unleashed in the believer's life, resulting in renewed faith, victory and *answered prayer.*

The prophet Jeremiah wrote, "Call unto me, and I will answer thee, and shew thee great and mighty things, which thou knowest not" (Jer. 33:3). Someone has pointed out that this passage (Jeremiah 33:3) is "God's telephone number" because it shows what happens when a true believer prays.

The principle behind this wonderful promise from God is quite simple. It is reaffirmed by the New Testament writer James who wrote: "Draw nigh to God, and he will draw nigh to you" (James 4:8). *God always responds to believing prayer!*

This book is based on this fundamental precept. The phenomenal power and presence of God are released in a person's life when he learns to personalize the promises of the Scriptures by offering them back to God through prayer. The results of this kind of praying are limitless. The Bible assures us that, "The effectual fervent prayer of a righteous man availeth much" (James 5:16). Praying the Word is effectual and it avails much in the believer's life because it builds faith in his heart. It activates God's supernatural power to meet our needs.

Alfred Lord Tennyson was "on target" when he wrote, "More things are wrought by prayer than this world dreams

9

of." In spite of this truth, which is backed up by countless prayer promises in the Word, many believers have failed to avail themselves of the boundless energy and infinite possibilities that come from praying the Word. Some may feel that their prayers are not answered. Others are overwhelmed by the circumstances of life. Too many times prayer becomes a last resort.

When the disciples begged, "Teach us to pray," the Lord gave them a model for effective praying:

> *When ye pray, say, Our Father which art in heaven, Hallowed be thy name. Thy kingdom come. Thy will be done, as in heaven, so in earth. Give us day by day our daily bread. And forgive us our sins; for we also forgive every one that is indebted to us. And lead us not into temptation; but deliver us from evil. (Luke 11:2-4)*

This brief prayer from the lips of Jesus has been called "The Lord's Prayer." It shows the essential ingredients that make the life of prayer work. His prayer opens with adoration of the Father and it reveals Jesus' earnest desire to pray in accord with the Father's will. In the Scriptures we find the will of God in its entirety. From this we may safely conclude that our praying will be effectual only when it closely adheres to the will of God as it is revealed through His Word.

The Apostle John confirms this: "And this is the confidence that we have in him, that, if we ask any thing *according to his will* he heareth us: And if we know that he hear us, whatsoever we ask, we know that we have the petitions that we desired of him" (1 John 5:14-15).

How do we know when we are praying according to the Father's will? Our prayers are always in line with the will of God *when we pray according to His Word*. Praying the Word of God brings answers to the human heart directly from the heart of God.

The basis for all the wonderful blessings we enjoy as children of the King — all the scriptural promises of answered prayer — is seen in the love of the Father for His children. John wrote, "Beloved let us love one another: for love is of God; and every one that loveth is born of God, and knoweth God. He that loveth not knoweth not God; for God is love" (1 John 4:7-8).

God loves you! There is no greater truth in the entire universe. Jesus said, "Ask, and it shall be given you; seek, and ye shall find; knock, and it shall be opened unto you. For every one that asketh receiveth; and he that seeketh findeth; and to him that knocketh it shall be opened. If a son shall ask bread of any of you that is a father, will he give him a stone? Or if he ask a fish, will he for a fish give him a serpent? Or if he shall ask an egg, will he offer him a scorpion? If ye then, being evil, know how to give good gifts unto your children: how much more shall your heavenly Father give the Holy Spirit to them that ask him?" (Luke 11:9-13). Both the power and love of God, through the Holy Spirit, invade your life when you pray according to the will of God as it has been revealed through His Word. He is there to sustain you and guide you. The Father's love is there to uphold you. Jesus, the Word made flesh, indwells your prayer life and He ever lives to make intercession for you according to the will of God.

The key to answered prayer is seen in Jesus' discourse on the true vine: "I am the true vine, and my Father is the husbandman. Every branch in me that beareth not fruit he taketh away: and every branch that beareth fruit, he purgeth it, that it may bring forth more fruit. Now ye are clean through the word which I have spoken unto you. Abide in me, and I in you. As the branch cannot bear fruit of itself, except it abide in the vine; no more can ye, except ye abide in me. I am the vine, ye are the branches: He that abideth in me, and I in him, the same bringeth forth much fruit: for without me ye can do nothing. If a man abide not in me, he is cast forth as a branch, and is withered; and men gather them, and cast them into the fire, and they are burned. If ye abide in me, *and my words abide in you,* ye shall ask what ye will, and it shall be done unto you" (John 15:1-7).

Notice how Jesus emphasized the importance of *His words abiding in our hearts as a prerequisite to answered prayer.* The value of this truth cannot be overemphasized; it is the absolute essential for effectual prayer. *We must learn to abide in Christ and to let His words abide in us!*

The topical prayers within this book have been developed with this command in mind: Abide in Christ and let His words abide in you; then you will ask what you will and it shall be done!

Praying the Word of God is not meant to serve as a reminder to God of all His precious prayer promises. He already knows them! Rather, this exciting, life-changing concept of prayer serves to remind us of His promises by building faith and expectation in our hearts. It keeps us in line with His will. This is what God wants for us because He loves us.

All of God's commandments stem from His love for us. He knows what is best for His children. When we fail to obey His Word, we always lose! His desire is for us to be victorious and the way to victory is found when we pray His Word.

Paul warned young Timothy to stay away from people who have "a form of godliness but (deny) the power thereof" (2 Tim. 3:5). The power of God is available to all who call upon Him in faith, for "without faith it is impossible to please God" (Heb. 11:6). Faith is released in the believer's life when he prays according to the will of God.

Paul also wrote, "The word is nigh thee, even in thy mouth, and in thy heart: that is, the word of faith, which we preach" (Rom. 10:8). Praying the Word of God expresses our faith to Him and it firmly establishes His Word in our hearts. Paul further explains the process in Romans 10:17: "Faith comes by hearing, and hearing by the word of God."

Prayer is our safe place — our place of refuge — in difficult times. "I am oftimes driven to my knees," wrote President Abraham Lincoln, "by the overwhelming conviction that I have nowhere else to go." The pressures and troubles of life have a way of bringing us to a renewed awareness of our need for the Father's help. The miracle of prayer is found in the truth that once we express our need(s) to the Father, He takes action in our behalf.

Arranged in a topical format, the prayers of this book are aimed at the needs of modern people in our fast-paced, anxiety-ridden age. The topics are covered by giving practical help to the reader through key thoughts, key Scriptures, faith-building prayers based on the Word of God, and additional Scriptures that give solid, concrete answers to life's dilemmas.

The prayers, for the most part, deal with commonalities we share as human beings who desire to follow Christ. The primary focus of the prayers is upon spiritual growth, victory over personal problems and ministry to others — matters of great concern to our loving Father and to us.

We have utilized the King James Version of the Holy Bible in most places throughout the book because this is the version with which most believers are familiar. The poetic language of the Authorized Version (KJV) lends itself beautifully to the language of heartfelt prayer. In a few places, for purposes of emphasis, we have utilized other translations as well. Except for purposes of clearer transitions between thoughts and ideas, we have endeavored to keep the wording of the prayers in original biblical form.

The uses of this book are as varied as the topics themselves. As a devotional aid, it will be a helpful tool in the hands of believers who want to draw closer to their Master. Beyond building familiarity with the Scriptures, the prayers are aimed at helping the believer know God, whom to know aright is life eternal. Counselors and personal workers who are involved in helping others will find this book to be a valuable reference in leading people to the throne of grace where they will find mercy and grace to help in their time of need (see Heb. 4:16). It is a book of comfort for those who are distressed, and a book of answers for those who are searching. Classes engaged in Bible study, and individuals involved in personal research will find the topical lists of Bible passages especially useful. What a marvelous giftbook it is to present to someone who wants to learn God's ways.

When you are lonely, these Scripture prayers bring the comfort of the Holy Spirit. The prayers impart hope to those who are experiencing despair and grief. Practical models for intercessory prayers in behalf of others are included as well. More than just a prayer book, this manual teaches the truths of God's Word, thereby enabling believers to stand upon the promises of God.

God has promised that His Word will not return unto Him void: "So shall my word be that goeth forth out of my mouth: it shall not return unto me void, but it shall accomplish that which I please, and it shall prosper in the thing whereto I sent it" (Isa. 55:11).

As we return God's Word to Him through prayer, we receive His answers because the Word of God is: "quick, and powerful, and sharper than any two-edged sword, piercing even to the dividing asunder of soul and spirit, and of the joints and marrow, and is a discerner of the thoughts and intents of the heart" (Heb. 4:12). As we learn to pray the Word, God reveals the motives of our hearts to us and we learn how to pray in accord with His will. God promises that His Word will then accomplish His will in our lives.

R.A. Torrey was a man of prayer. He wrote, "Mere intellectual study of the Word of God is not enough; there must be meditation upon it. The Word of God must be revolved over and over in the mind with a constant looking to God and His Spirit to make that Word a living thing in the heart. The prayer that is born of meditation on the Word of God is the prayer which soars upward to God's listening ear.

"George Mueller, one of the mightiest men of prayer, would begin praying by reading and meditating upon God's Word until a prayer began to form itself in his heart. Thus, God himself was the real author of the prayer, and God answered the prayer which He himself had inspired.

"The Word of God is the instrument through which the Holy Spirit works. It is the sword of the Spirit in more senses than one. The person who wants to know the work of the Holy Spirit in any direction must feed upon the Word. The person who desires to pray in the Spirit must meditate on the Word, so that the Holy Spirit may have something through which He can work. The Holy Spirit works His prayers in us through the Word. Neglect of the Word makes praying in the Holy Spirit an impossibility. If we seek to feed the fire of our prayers with the fuel of God's Word, all our difficulties in prayer will disappear" (From *How to Pray* by R.A. Torrey).

When we meditate upon God's Word and pray His thoughts, we experience the delight of knowing His ways.

The Scriptures promise, "Blessed is the man that walketh not in the counsel of the ungodly, nor standeth in the way of sinners, nor sitteth in the seat of the scornful. But *his delight is in the law of the Lord; and in his law doth he meditate day and night.* And he shall be like a tree planted by the rivers of water, that bringeth forth his fruit in his season; his leaf also shall not wither; and whatsoever he doeth shall prosper" (Ps. 1:1-3).

Can there be any better way? The prophet Isaiah pointed out the great gulf between God's thoughts and ours: "For my thoughts are not your thoughts, neither are your ways my ways, saith the Lord" (Isa. 55:11). Praying the Word of God and meditating upon His thoughts bridges the gap between our humanity and the divinity of the Lord. As we express His thoughts in prayer we learn to walk in His ways.

In the case of George Mueller, we know that his prayers in accord with God's Word brought miraculous results. Expressing his needs and the needs of his orphans to God alone through faith brought everything that was required for daily provision and it ushered countless souls into the Kingdom of God.

Mueller's prayer life was a powerful, living affirmation of the truth of James 1:6-8: "But let him ask in faith, nothing wavering. For he that wavereth is like a wave of the sea driven with the wind and tossed. For let not that man think that he shall receive any thing of the Lord. A double minded man is unstable in all his ways" (James 1:6-8).

As noted earlier, faith comes through the Word of God. By praying that Word, we cease our wavering and we learn to believe that God will accomplish His Word in our lives.

Jesus assures us of this truth: "What things soever ye desire, when ye pray, believe that ye receive them, and ye shall have them" (Mark 11:24). Listen to the words of another great prayer warrior, Andrew Murray, who wrote: "The more heartily we enter into the mind of our blessed Lord, simply thinking about prayer as He thought, the more surely His words will become living seeds. They will grow and produce their fruit in us — a life corresponding exactly to the Divine truth they contain. Do let us believe this: Christ, the living Word of God, gives, in His words, a Divine quickening power which brings what they say, which works in us what He asks, and which actually enables us to do everything He demands" (From *The Ministry of Intercession* by Andrew Murray.)

Praying the Word of God leads us to walking in the Word of God. The will of God becomes our greatest delight, as was the case with the Psalmist who wrote, "I delight to do thy will, O my God: yea, thy law is within my heart" (Ps. 40:8).

E.M. Bounds elaborates on this theme in his book, *The Necessity of Prayer:* "Prayer draws its very life from the Bible. It places its security on the firm ground of Scripture. Its very existence and character depend on revelation made by God to man in His holy Word. Prayer, in turn, exalts this same revelation and turns men toward that Word. The nature, necessity, and all-comprehending character of prayer is based on the Word of God."

The power of prayer flows from the Word of God. "He that cometh to God must believe that he is, and that he is a rewarder of them that diligently seek him" (Heb. 11:6). This kind of faith comes from the revelation of the Word to our hearts. It is the kind of faith that God always rewards. Meditating on that Word, and praying its truths, reinforces our belief in God as our rewarder.

It has been said that "Satan trembles when he sees the weakest saint upon his knees." The devil is cunning and he feels successful when he keeps us from prayer. In times of prayerlessness, the devil is enabled to lay traps that will cause us to stumble and fall. As Andrew Bonar pointed out, "The one concern of Satan is to keep the saints from prayer. He fears nothing from prayerless studies, prayerless work, prayerless religion. He laughs at our toil, mocks at our wisdom, and trembles when we pray." This is even more true as we learn to pray more and more effectually.

We must pray the Word of God because this is our sure defense against the enemy. Paul wrote, "Finally, my brethren, be strong in the Lord, and in the power of his might. Put on the whole armor of God, that ye may be able to stand against the wiles of the devil. For we wrestle not against flesh and blood, but against principalities, against powers, against the rulers of the darkness of this world, against spiritual wickedness in high places. Wherefore take unto you the whole armour of God, that ye may be able to withstand in the evil day, and having done all, to stand. Stand therefore, having your loins girt about with truth, and having on the breastplate of righteousness; And your feet shod with the preparation of the gospel of peace; Above all, taking the shield of faith, wherewith ye shall be able to quench all the fiery darts of the wicked. And take the helmet of salvation, and *the sword of the Spirit, which is the word of God; praying always with all prayer and supplication in the Spirit,* and watching thereunto with all perseverance and supplication..." (Eph. 6:11-18).

The sword of the Spirit is the Word of God. It is made effectual by praying always with all prayer and supplication in the Spirit. The two are inseparable. The armor of God is incomplete if it is not put on with prayer.

PERSONALIZING THE WORD IN PRAYER

The first step, then, in this exciting process of power-packed praying is to personalize the Word of God in our hearts. Five personal questions may be employed to help us do this:

1. What does the passage teach me about Jesus Christ?

2. Is there any error in this passage for me to avoid?

3. Is there any command in this passage for me to obey?

4. Is there any example in this passage for me to follow?

5. Is there any promise in this passage for me to claim?

Your answers to these questions form the framework for effectual prayers based on the Word of God. Although this book stresses the promises of God, many of the prayers reflect also on His commandments, the examples of Bible characters, the life of our Lord and the sins and errors that become pitfalls in the believer's life.

The prayers foster an intimate, personal relationship with the Lord Jesus Christ. He is addressed with the personal pronoun "you," and the wording of each prayer is conversational in tone.

Many of the prayers utilize verses from the Book of Psalms because these beautiful songs are very personal and they deal with most of the doctrines and concepts that are important to Christians.

Psalms 42 serves as an excellent example to help us in developing personalized prayer:

> *As the hart panteth after the water brooks, so panteth my soul after thee, O God. My soul thirsteth for God, for the living God; when shall I come and appear before God? My tears have been my meat day and night, while they continually say unto me, Where is thy God? When I remember these things, I pour out my soul in me: for I had gone with the multitude, I went with them to the house of God, with the voice of joy and praise, with a multitude that kept holyday. Why art thou cast down, O my soul? and why art thou disquieted in me? hope thou in God: for I shall yet praise him for the help of his countenance. O my God, my soul is cast down within me: therefore will I remember thee from the land of Jordan, and of the Hermonites, from the hill Mizar. Deep calleth unto deep at the noise of thy waterspouts: all the waves and the billows are gone over me. Yet the Lord will command his lovingkindness in the daytime, and in the night his song shall be with me, and my prayer unto the God of my life. I will say unto God my rock, Why hast thou forgotten me? Why go I mourning because of the oppression of the enemy? As with a sword in my bones, mine enemies reproach me; while they say daily unto me, Where is thy God? Why art thou cast down, O my soul? and why art thou disquieted within me? hope thou in God; for I shall yet praise him, who is the health of my countenance, and my God.*

This psalm comes forth from the author's heart-cry. It is intensely personal and it deals with the themes of spiritual hunger, depression, discouragement, and rejection. By reflecting on the nature of God and His wonderful lovingkindness, however, the Psalmist is able to end his prayer with a note of hope and joy, rooted deeply in confidence in God. The same thing will happen to you as you learn to pray the Word by personalizing its truths to your circumstances.

Let's see how this revolutionary concept of prayer works with Psalms 42. *What does this passage teach me about Jesus Christ?* Although His name is not mentioned, we know from other passages that He has been with the Father since the beginning. Therefore, when the Psalmist refers to "the Lord," we can make applications of his statements to our Lord Jesus Christ.

What attributes of Jesus are reflected in this Psalm? The author refers to the "living God." He is alive! His lovingkindness is available to the Psalmist in the daytime and His song is with the Psalmist during the night. The Lord is the God of his life and his rock. The Lord is the health of his countenance.

When we make those thoughts personal by applying them to our own lives, we see who God is and how wonderful He is to us. He is the living God to *me.* His lovingkindness is with *me* in the daytime. His song is with *me* at night. He is the God of *my* life. He is *my* rock. The Lord is the health of *my* countenance. What power there is in the realization of who the Lord Jesus Christ really is! Who He is to *me*!

In prayer, then, we can acknowledge these attributes as follows:

> *Lord, you are the living God. Your lovingkindness is with me in the daytime, and your song is with me at night. You are the God of my life and you are my rock. You are the health of my countenance. Praise your holy name!*

Doesn't that prayer build faith and power in your heart? It is thoroughly scriptural and it imparts the power of the Word. By meditating on these qualities of our Lord we soon see that the problems of life pale to insignificance in the light of His glory.

Is there any error in this passage for me to avoid? The primary error is both implied and stated. The Psalmist recalls his tears and this leads him down the dark alley of depression. He loses hope. He grows slightly paranoid

about others, especially the ones he considers to be his
enemies. Or, perhaps, as often happens with believers today,
it is not human enemies, but the enemy — the deceiver
and accuser — whose whisperings the Psalmist is battling,
with less-than-total success. Whatever the case, he loses
sight of the power of God when he dwells on his problems
and feelings. Obviously these errors in his thinking and
behavior are in opposition to the will of God for him.
Through the Psalmist's honest sharing about his feelings,
we learn to avoid his errors, and this is how we may pray:

> *Lord, I know it is not your will for my tears to be*
> *my meat both day and night. Why are you cast down, O*
> *my soul? Why are you disquieted within me? Deep calls*
> *unto deep at the noise of your waterspouts. All your waves*
> *and billows overwhelm me. I will hope in my God, for you*
> *are my only hope. I will yet praise you, for you are the*
> *health of my countenance, and my God.*

In the above personalized, scriptural prayer, we
express our need to God by honestly sharing with Him our
feelings and the errors in our thinking, but as the Psalmist
did, we conclude our cry with a note of confidence, trust
and praise. In so doing, we are taken from the depths of
depression into the wonderful realm of God's glory and
victory.

Is there any command in this passage for me to obey?
There is really only one direct command in this chapter:
"Hope thou in God." The Psalmist repeats it twice and
each time he backs it up with a personal commitment:
"...for I shall yet praise him for the help of his
countenance," and "for I shall yet praise him, who is the
health of my countenance and my God." Making personal
application of these verses to our own prayer life is quite
simple yet utterly profound:

> *Lord, I will hope in you. You are my God. I command*
> *my soul to hope in you, for you are the health of my*
> *countenance and my God. I will praise you for the help*
> *of your countenance. O Lord, you are my rock.*

That is powerful praying, and when used appropriately, it is liberating and faith-building.

Notice the positive direction these prayers are taking as we continue our process. *Is there any example for me to follow in this passage?* The author of Psalms 42 provides us with several examples to follow: his soul pants after God, he is honest with his feelings and his doubts, he remembers good times in the house of God, he commits himself to hoping in God and praising Him, and he promises to pray to the God of his life. Each of these examples is worthy of emulation in our lives, and together they lead us to pray:

> *Father, my soul pants after you like the deer pants after streams of water. I am thirsty for you. I remember the times when I went to your house and joined in with your people in joy and praise. But, Lord, I am struggling with sadness. My tears have been my meat both night and day. I know this is not your will for me. I will hope in you because you are the God of my life, my very rock. You have promised to command your lovingkindness in the daytime and your song will be with me tonight as I pray unto you, O Lord. I will yet praise you for you are the health of my countenance and my God. Hallelujah!*

Instead of dwelling on the negative, the individual turns to God, who embodies hope and confidence. When we turn our eyes on Jesus, the things of earth do grow strangely dim and the light of His Word provides a clearly marked path for our lives.

Is there any promise in this passage for me to claim? There are several: God is the living God. We will appear before Him. His countenance helps us. He will command His lovingkindness in the daytime. He will give us a song at night. He will be the health of our countenance, and our God.

We pray these promises back to Him so we will remember them and act upon them through faith:

*Lord Jesus, you are the living God. You have
promised that we will one day appear before you. Until
that wonderful day arrives, you have promised to command
your lovingkindness in the daytime and your song at night.
You will be the health of my countenance and my God.*

These are important points to review over and over
again. They are uplifting and comforting thoughts. They
are a gift of God's love to you and me.

Every passage of the Scriptures can be dissected in
this way and applied to our daily lives and prayers. As Paul
reminded Timothy: "All scripture is given by inspiration
of God, and is profitable for doctrine, for reproof, for
correction, for instruction in righteousness: That the man
of God may be perfect, thoroughly furnished unto all good
works" (2 Tim. 3:16-17).

As in all things, the Bible is the light by which we
pray. "Thy word is a lamp to my feet, and a light unto my
path" (Ps. 119:105). As Kenyon Palmer called it, "God's
road map — the Bible." God's Book is a manual for learning
the life of prayer. Using God's words as the skeletal matter
for our prayers enables us to pray with His power, His
direction and His wisdom. It gives us His answers even
while we pray.

John Bunyan wrote, "Prayer is a sincere, sensible,
affectionate pouring out of the soul to God through Christ
in the strength and assistance of the Spirit, for such things
as God has promised." We find those promises in the Word
of God and to pray that Word brings us the strength of
Christ and the power of the Holy Spirit.

"To pray well is the better half of study," wrote Martin
Luther. Study of the Word of God leads us to pray according
to His ways. Paul's words to Timothy apply both to prayer
and to study: "Study to shew thyself approved unto God,
a workman that needeth not to be ashamed, rightly dividing
the word of truth" (2 Tim. 2:15). By praying the Word we

learn to divide His truth rightly. The well-known missionary, Frank C. Laubach, pointed to this correlation when he wrote, "Prayer at its highest is a two-way conversation — and for me the most important part is listening to God's replies." Herein is the beauty and the power of praying from and in the Word of God — we do receive answers!

We conclude our introduction to this book on Scripture praying with a prayer for you from the Scriptures: "Let the word of Christ dwell in you richly in all wisdom...And whatsoever ye do in word or deed, do all in the name of the Lord Jesus, giving thanks to God and the Father by him" (Col. 3:16-17).

As R.A. Torrey pointed out, the scriptural promises of prayer are based on the principle that: "If we are to receive from God all we ask from Him, Christ's words must abide in us. We must study His words and let them sink into our thoughts and heart. We must keep them in our memory, obey them constantly in our life, and let them shape and mold our daily life and our every act.

"This is really the method of abiding in Christ. It is through His words that Jesus imparts Himself to us. The words He speaks unto us, they are spirit and they are life (John 6:63). It is vain to expect power in prayer unless we meditate upon the words of Christ and let them sink deep and find a permanent abode in our hearts. There are many who wonder why they are so powerless in prayer. The very simple explanation of it all is found in their neglect of the words of Christ. They have not hidden His words in their hearts; His words do not abide in them. It is not by moments of mystical meditation and rapturous experiences that we learn to abide in Christ. It is by feeding upon His Word, His written word in the Bible, and looking to the Spirit to implant these words in our heart — to thus make them a living thing in our heart. If we thus let the words of Christ abide in us, they will stir us up to prayer. *They will be the mold in which our prayers are shaped.* And, our prayers will necessarily be along the line of God's will and will prevail with Him. Prevailing prayer is almost an impossibility where there is neglect of the study of God's Word" (From *How to Pray* by R.A. Torrey).

Our prayer is that this book will help you to learn to shape your prayers according to the Word of God. By doing this, you will find your prayers becoming *PRAYERS THAT PREVAIL*. Remember that He will hear you, and He will answer!

KEYS TO ANSWERED PRAYER

Jesus said, "Ask, and it shall be given you; seek, and ye shall find; knock, and it shall be opened unto you" (Matt. 7:7). Sometimes people seem to feel that answers to their prayers are securely locked behind an impenetrable wall. They may feel that they have knocked on God's door without obtaining the answers they seek.

The Scriptures are replete with promises of answered prayer, however, and a careful look at the teachings of Jesus reveals certain keys we may employ to open the door leading to the abundant riches of His glory. The Father wants to answer our prayers, but first we must learn the principles of prayer He has outlined as the ways and means by which we get His answers.

Key #1 — PRAYING ACCORDING TO THE WILL OF GOD

Faith that God will answer your prayers is cultivated by adhering to biblical principles that do not fail. The keys to answered prayer are available for the use of every believer.

Praying according to the will of God is one of those keys. It brings us everything God wants us to have. It is a prayer rooted in the confidence that God hears us and that He wants to answer us. This exciting principle is revealed by the Apostle John:

> *And this is the confidence that we have in him, that,*
> *if we ask any thing according to his will, he heareth us:*
> *And if we know that he hear us, whatsoever we ask, we*

27

know that we have the petition that we desired of him.
(1 John 5:14-15)

How do we determine His will so we are enabled to pray with such confidence? This knowledge is a direct result of familiarity with God's Word and the indwelling of God's Spirit. We must fill our hearts with divine precepts from the Bible in order to be in tune with the will of God. In so doing we learn what God wants, and we shape our prayers accordingly.

It is as E.M. Bounds wrote, "To know God's will in prayer, we must be filled with God's Spirit, who makes intercession for the saints according to the will of God. To be filled with God's Spirit, to be filled with God's Word, is to know God's will. It is to be put in such a frame of mind and state of heart that it will enable us to read and correctly interpret the purposes of the infinite. Such filling of the heart with the Word and the Spirit gives us an insight into the will of the Father. It enables us to rightly discern His will and puts a disposition of mind and heart within us to make it the guide and compass of our lives" (From *The Necessity of Prayer* by E.M. Bounds).

Familiarity with the Word of God and praying from the perspective of His Word produce phenomenal changes both in our praying and our living. It affects all that we say, think and do. This style of prayer calls the power of God, through the Holy Spirit, into action in our behalf.

Praying according to the will of God changes things. Most importantly, it enables us to *accept* the will of God even if His will is different from what we may have originally hoped. Jesus said, "If ye abide in me, and my words abide in you, ye shall ask what ye will, and it shall be done unto you" (John 15:7). When the words of our Lord find their abode within our hearts, our will becomes one with His. It is in conforming our will to the Father's (through the operation of the Spirit and the Word) that we know our prayers will be answered.

Key #2 — PRAYING IN THE NAME OF JESUS

The name of Jesus is above every name. It speaks of the power and authority of God. To pray in His name is to pray with full assurance that everything His name represents will bring God's answers to our needs.

"In Jesus' name" is a phrase that is frequently attached to prayer as a complimentary close. Although this is certainly an appropriate practice, it does not come close to the meaning of Jesus when He told us to pray in His name. In effect, He was giving us the power of attorney to represent Him — and all He possesses — by praying in His name. To pray in the name of Jesus is to pray in the full realization of who He is, what He stands for, what He is able to do, and what He wants. We are representing Him when we are praying in His name, and so we must be sure that our prayers are in agreement with Him.

What a privilege it is to know that we can pray with His authority as it is represented by His name. At the mention of His name (when spoken in faith), the demons flee. Every knee shall bow at the mention of His name.

Six times in the gospels Jesus reiterated the importance of praying in His name. In His discourse on divine comfort He explained the reasons for doing so:

> *Verily, verily, I say unto you, He that believeth on me, the works that I do shall he do also; and greater works than these shall he do; because I go unto my Father. And whatsoever ye shall ask in my name, that will I do, that the Father may be glorified in the Son. If ye shall ask anything in my name, I will do it. (John 14:12-14).*

Foretelling His ascension to the right hand of the Father, Jesus revealed the power of His name in prayer.

He gave us the legal right to use His name in prayer because we were to become His representatives on earth. Clearly, God's power is unleashed in the believer's life when he uses the name of Jesus in full realization of who He is, what He has accomplished and what He will do. Through proper use of His name in prayer, we will accomplish great works and the Father will be glorified.

Andrew Murray wrote, "He (the Lord Jesus) longed so much for us to really believe that His Name is the power in which every knee should bow, and in which every prayer could be heard, that he did not weary of saying it over and over: 'In My name.' Between the wonderful *whatsoever ye shall ask, and the Divine I will do it, the Father will give it,* the simple link is: 'In My name.' Our asking and the Father's giving are equal in the Name of Christ. Everything in prayer depends upon our comprehending this: 'In My name.' " (From *The Ministry of Intercession* by Andrew Murray.)

The following verses reveal other important truths about praying in the name of Jesus:

> *I have chosen you...that whatsoever ye shall ask of the Father in my name, He may give it you. (John 15:16)*

> *Verily, verily, I say unto you, Whatsoever ye shall ask the Father in my name, He will give it you. Hitherto have ye asked nothing in my name; ask, and ye shall receive, that your joy may be full. (John 16:23-24)*

Jesus has chosen you to go forth and bear much fruit so that the Father will be glorified! Praying in the Name of Jesus brings forth much fruit.

Jesus wants you to experience fullness of joy! Notice how praying in His name brings this to pass: You will receive, and your joy will be full!

Key #3 — **PRAYING IN FAITH, NOTHING WAVERING**

But let him ask in faith, nothing wavering For he that wavereth is like a wave of the sea driven with the wind and tossed. For let not that man think that he shall receive any thing of the Lord. A double minded man is unstable in all his ways. (James 1:6-8)

There is no doubt about it: we must ask in faith, nothing wavering. We must, as the writer to the Hebrews stated, believe that God is and that He is a rewarder of all those who come to Him in faith. The Scriptures are clear about this: "Without faith it is impossible to please him [God]" (Heb. 11:6).

Jesus put it this way: "Therefore I say unto you, What things soever ye desire when ye pray, *believe* that ye receive them, and ye shall have them" (Mark 11:24).

God has given us many promises. He is faithful and trustworthy. Our responsibility is to respond to His ability to do what He says. Faith tells us, "God cannot fail"; "Nothing is impossible with God." Unless we activate that faith in our hearts, however, God is not able to move.

Charles Haddon Spurgeon developed a helpful analogy to give us insight into praying in faith. He wrote, "Faith goes up the stairs that love has made and looks out of the windows which hope has opened."

Think of the potential inherent in a prayer life that appropriates and acts upon these words of Jesus:

If ye have faith as a grain of mustard seed, ye shall say unto this mountain, Remove hence to yonder place; and it shall remove; and nothing shall be impossible unto you.

(Matthew 17:20)

Key #4 — **PERSISTENCE IN PRAYER**

From time to time all of us are tempted to give up. We grow weary of the journey. On the night of His betrayal Jesus spent several hours in persistent, agonizing prayer. He invited His disciples to join Him, but soon they grew weary and fell asleep. When the Lord found them sleeping, He expressed His disappointment and concern to them, "Why sleep ye? Rise and pray, lest ye enter into temptation" (Luke 22:46).

Persistence in prayer in the Garden of Gethsemane caused our Lord to agonize over the unavoidable issues He knew He must face. "And being in agony he prayed more earnestly: and his sweat was as it were great drops of blood falling down to the ground" (Luke 22:44). While the disciples were sleeping, their Master was sweating blood in persistent prayer. What a contrast!

"He found them sleeping *for sorrow*." Have you ever experienced being so burdened, overwrought or overwhelmed that you just wanted to go to bed and stay there — or go off someplace and die? That is sleeping for sorrow. And that is the reaction of the flesh nature to stress. But we need to learn to recognize that feeling as a call to earnest, persistent prayer. How true it often is that the storm is darkest just before the dawn. But often the dawn never comes in our prayer life because we quit and go to sleep just before the victory is won.

An anonymous writer describes persistence in prayer as follows: "How glibly we talk of praying without ceasing! Yet, we are quite ready to quit if our prayer remains unanswered but a week or a month! We assume that by a stroke of His arm or an action of His will, God will give us what we ask. It never seems to dawn on us that He is the Master of nature, as of grace, and that, sometimes He chooses one way, and sometimes another, to do His work. It takes years, sometimes, to answer a prayer. When it is answered, we can look back to see that it did take years. But God knows all the time. It is His will that we pray, and pray, and still pray, and so come to know indeed what it is to pray without ceasing."

Jesus said that "men ought always to pray and not to faint" (Luke 18:1). James wrote, "The effectual, fervent prayer of a righteous man availeth much" (James 5:16). Paul wrote, "Pray without ceasing" (1 Thess. 5:17). In telling the story of the persistent widow, Jesus pointed out, "And shall not God avenge His own elect, which cry day and night unto Him, though He bear long with them? I tell you He will avenge them speedily" (Luke 18:1-8).

Key #5 — BEING SPECIFIC IN PRAYER

Our prayers cannot be effective if they are vague and general. We need to make our prayers specific and definite. Jesus said, "Whosoever...shall not doubt in his heart, but shall believe that those things which he saith shall come to pass; he shall have whatsoever he saith" (Mark 11:23).

Again we see the importance of faith, but it is a specific faith for specific things. For our answers to be definite, we need to make our requests definite.

To pray "bless my friend" is a far less effective prayer than "bless my friend with _____," listing the specific needs of his/her life. The same principle applies to our prayer life whether we are praying for our own needs or the needs of another.

E. M. Bounds wrote, "Faith and prayer select the subjects to be prayed for thus determining what God is to do. 'He shall have whatsoever he saith.' Christ is ready to supply exactly and fully all the demands of faith and of prayer. If the order to God is clear, specific, and definite, God will fit it exactly in agreement with the terms put before Him."

"Be careful for nothing; but in every thing by prayer and supplication with thanksgiving let your requests be made known unto God" (Phil. 4:6). Specific things — specific requests. The result will be: "And the peace of God, which passeth all understanding, shall keep your hearts and minds through Christ Jesus" (Phil. 4:7).

Key #6 — PRAYING IN HUMILITY

Brokenness is the condition of life that reveals to us our spiritual needs. It leads us to express our needs to the Father without question, for we know truly that we have nowhere else to go. God responds to the prayer that emanates from the humble in heart, those who have been broken from their self-will and their need to control everything.

The Psalmist wrote, "O Lord, open thou my lips; and my mouth shall shew forth thy praise... The sacrifices of God are a broken spirit; a broken and contrite heart, O God, thou wilt not despise" (Ps. 51:15&17).

Fenelon wrote, "Leave it all to God; it is not your business to judge how He should deal with you, because He knows far better than you what is good for you. You deserve a certain amount of trial and dryness. Bear it patiently! God does his part...Try to do yours too, and that is to love Him without waiting for Him to testify His love for you."

God loves to bless the humble in heart. It is wise for us to reflect often on these Old Testament words: "If my people, which are called by my name, shall humble themselves, and pray, and seek my face, and turn from their wicked ways; then will I hear from heaven, and will forgive their sin, and will heal their land" (2 Chron. 7:14).

Key #7 — PRAYING IN THE SPIRIT

The Holy Spirit is our life. His breath fills us with the life and power of God. To pray in the Spirit, therefore, is to pray in power. It is life-changing and life-producing prayer.

Paul wrote, "With all prayer and supplication in the Spirit, and watching thereunto with all perseverance and supplication for all the saints" (Eph. 6:18). The Holy Spirit is a Spirit of prayer. "He maketh intercession for the saints according to the will of God" (Rom. 8:26). In *The Ministry of Intercession,* Andrew Murray writes, " 'I will pour out the Spirit of supplication.' Are you beginning to see that the mystery of prayer is the mystery of the Divine indwelling? God in heaven gives His Spirit to be the Divine power praying in our hearts, drawing us upward to our God. God is a Spirit, and nothing but a similar life and Spirit within us can have communion with Him. Man was created for this communion with God, so that God could dwell and work in him, and be the life of his life. It was the Divine indwelling that sin lost. Christ came to exhibit it in His life, to win it back for us in His death, and then to impart it to us by coming again from heaven in the Spirit to live in His disciples. Only this indwelling of God through the Spirit can explain and enable us to appropriate the wonderful promises given to prayer. God gives the Spirit as a Spirit of supplication, too, to maintain His Divine life within us as a life in which prayer continually rises to heaven."

It is the Holy Spirit who helps us when we pray. He brings to our remembrance the things that Jesus has taught us and He empowers us for the important ministry of intercession. He prays for us in "groanings that cannot be uttered" (See Romans 8). To pray effectively, then, we must be filled with the Spirit of God.

> *But if the Spirit of him that raised up Jesus from the dead dwell in you, he that raised up Christ from the dead shall also quicken your mortal bodies by his Spirit that dwelleth in You...ye have received the Spirit of adoption, whereby we cry, Abba, Father. (Rom. 8:11-15)*

Key #8 — WAITING ON GOD

One fruit of the Spirit of God is longsuffering (or patience). Patience comes, also, through the life of prayer. We do not want to get ahead of God nor to lag behind Him, for we know that His timing is perfect.

Prayer gives us the grace to wait on God — to wait for Him — to wait in His presence.

> *But let patience have her perfect work, that ye may be perfect and entire, wanting nothing. (James 1:4)*

Sometimes God doesn't give us what we ask for immediately because He knows we're not ready for it. A time of preparation is called for. The process is one of development into perfection (wholeness, completion), and it begins with prayer.

The Psalmist wrote, "My soul, wait only upon God" (Ps. 62:1). Jesus charged His disciples not to "depart from Jerusalem, but to wait for the promise of the Father" (Acts 1:4). How easily we are tempted to do anything but wait. Oftentimes the Scriptures admonish us to "stand still," "be still," "wait," "stand fast," "set yourself." In essence, we are advised to slow down and give God time to do His wonderful work.

This is the meaning of "waiting on God," and we see it elucidated further by Andrew Murray:

> *'Take heed, and be quiet: fear not, neither be faint-hearted.' 'In quietness and in confidence shall be your strength.' Such words reveal to us the close connection between quietness and faith. They show us what a deep need there is of quietness, the element of true waiting upon*

God. If we are to have our whole heart turned toward God, we must have it turned away from man, from all that occupies and interests, whether of joy or sorrow. (From *Waiting On God* by Andrew Murray.)

There is peace in waiting upon God, and there is the development of patience. Best of all, it brings us a quiet assurance that God will answer in the best possible manner.

Thou shalt know that I am the Lord: for they shall not be ashamed that wait for me. (Isa. 49:23)

Blessed are all they that wait for him. (Isa. 30:18).

Key #9 — THANKSGIVING AND PRAISE

Two very important elements of an effective prayer life are thanksgiving and praise. Oftentimes, they bring immediate answers to the needs of our hearts. Thanksgiving, for example, lifts us out of the doldrums of depression and discouragement by helping us to focus on the blessings God has given to us. The hymn says it well, "Count your blessings, name them one by one, and it will surprise you what the Lord has done." It's all a matter of focus. We can get our eyes on the problems or on the One who can solve them. Needless to say, the latter alternative is the better one.

It is praise that enables us to get our eyes on Jesus, leading us into true worship. We see Him as He really is — the Lord of the universe, the One who possesses all power in heaven and in earth. He is the Rewarder of all who diligently seek Him (see Heb. 11:6).

Terry Law puts it well:

When Christians begin to pray, they often feel far off from God, that God is distant. They can be absolutely correct in their doctrine and have a good grasp of Scripture, but they have no sense of fellowship with God. They don't really know Him intimately...The Scripture is very clear in telling us that praise is the only avenue of

access to God...The way through the gate is thanksgiving;
the way into the court is praise. If we want to enter, there
is no other way. (From *The Power of Praise and Worship*
by Terry Law.)

The Scriptures give solid support to this admonition about thanksgiving and praise. Listen to the words of the Psalmist: "Enter into His gates with thanksgiving, and into His courts with praise: be thankful unto him, and bless his name" (Ps 100:4).

Key #10 — **ABIDING IN CHRIST**

Well-known author Oswald Chambers writes, "It is the dull, bald, dreary, commonplace day, with commonplace duties and people, that kills the burning heart unless we have learned the secret of abiding in Jesus." Jesus is our safe place, our refuge from the storms of life; but the key to getting our prayers answered is not found in fleeing to Jesus when the times get tough — the key works best when we learn to live in Him, to stay there, knowing that He is our abode, our resting place, our home. In Him we live and move and have our being. In Him all things find their completion and all things hold together. Abiding in Christ brings answers to our prayers.

Jesus wrote, "Abide in me, and I in you. As the branch cannot bear fruit of itself, except it abide in the vine; no more can ye, except ye abide in me. ...If ye abide in me, and my words abide in you, ye shall ask what ye will, and it shall be done unto you" (John 15:4&7).

Please note the two conditions Jesus gives as a means for getting our prayers answered: *we must abide in Him and we must let His words abide in us.*

In *The Practice of the Presence of God*, Brother Lawrence speaks to the integral need of abiding in Christ:

The first blessing that the soul receives from the practice of the presence of God is that its faith is livelier and more active everywhere in our lives. This is particularly true in difficult times, since it obtains the grace we need to deal with temptation and to conduct ourselves in the world. The soul — accustomed by this exercise to the practice of faith — can actually see and feel God by simply entering His presence. It envokes Him easily and obtains what it needs. In so doing, the soul could be said to approach the Blessed, in that it can almost say, 'I no longer believe, but I see and experience.' Its faith becomes more and more penetrating as it advances through practice.

Abiding in Christ is prayer without ceasing. It is the life of prayer, and the natural outgrowth of such a life always involves getting God's answers. Prayer becomes "the soul's sincere desire, the Christian's native air," and God's answers come naturally in our daily walk.

We have outlined but a few of the scriptural principles that lead to answered prayer. The important thing to realize is that when they are applied on a daily basis in our lives they bring results. If we follow these precepts, our prayers cannot fail; our prayers will become *PRAYERS THAT PREVAIL.*

THE MODEL PRAYER OF JESUS

Jesus wants you to learn to pray with power so that your prayers can effect positive changes in your life and in the lives of others for whom you pray. When His disciples asked Him to teach them how to pray, Jesus responded by giving them a model prayer to serve as the framework on which to build a life of prayer. This model prayer has come to be known as "The Lord's Prayer," and it is used in many churches today as a regular part of Sunday morning services. This model prayer of Jesus, however, is so much more than a ritual form to be repeated on Sunday mornings; rather, it is a practical outline of prayer's essential components presented by our Lord to lead us into a meaningful relationship with the Father from whom all blessings flow.

One style of teaching used with great success by first-century rabbis was to present an important concept by listing all its inherent principles and related topics in outline form, point by point. The Lord's Prayer is such an outline, presented by Jesus to show us how to pray effectively. As we learn to build our prayers on the framework provided by this model prayer, we discover exciting principles that have the potential to revolutionize the way we pray and the way we get answers to our prayers. *"After this manner therefore pray ye..."* (Matt. 6:9).

> *Our Father which art in heaven, Hallowed be thy name. Thy kingdom come. Thy will be done in earth, as it is in heaven. Give us this day our daily bread. And forgive us our debts, as we forgive our debtors. And lead us not into temptation, but deliver us from evil. For thine*

*is the kingdom, and the power, and the glory, forever.
Amen. (Matt. 6:9-13)*

We will focus on nine of the prayer principles outlined
by Jesus in His model prayer, then we will develop a
personal prayer based on these nine vital elements.

I. *Our Father which art in heaven.* Viewing God as
our Father changes everything, including our understanding
of prayer. It changes the way we see God, ourselves, other
people and the world.

Much can be learned about prayer by observing the
way a child relates to a caring father. When the child is
hurt, frightened or discouraged, he goes to his dad in the
firm confidence that his father will be able to help him.
When a valued possession — such as a favorite toy — is
broken, he asks dad to fix it. He *simply believes* in his
father's ability to make things better.

This child-like trust, simplicity and expectation are
essential elements in effective praying. As in all things,
Jesus gives us the perfect example: "Abba, Father, all things
are possible unto thee" (Mark 14:36). This all-
encompassing faith is an absolute prerequisite to prevailing
in prayer. All things are possible to our heavenly Father!

In the same way that the child's father does all within
his power to help his youngster, our heavenly Father
responds to our trust, love and faith by meeting our needs
in supernatural ways. This principle of effective prayer is
further elucidated in the Book of Hebrews: "But without
faith it is impossible to please him: for he that cometh to
God must believe that he is, and that he is a rewarder of
them that diligently seek him" (Heb. 11:6).

Through prayer we foster an intimate relationship with
our heavenly Father. We learn what He's like and we
discover His ways. He reveals His will to us and He tells

us what He expects of us. From this trusting relationship with our Father in heaven we receive all that we need.

II. *Hallowed be thy name.* The word "hallowed" is best defined by its synonyms: holy, consecrated, revered and sacred. In His model prayer, Jesus expresses reverence for His Father by giving special regard to His names. The names of God in the Bible reveal His attributes. They tell us many important things about His nature. By reflecting on the names of God, as Jesus did in the Lord's Prayer, we are reminded of who God is, how He works in our lives, and the blessings He has promised to impart to His children.

Let's review the meanings of the names of God and apply them to our understanding of prayer:

1. *Yahweh/Jehovah* — The God who always is and never changes.
2. *Adonai* — the Lord who is eternal.
3. *Jehovah-Elohim* — the majestic Lord who is worthy of worship.
4. *Jehovah-Elyon* — the Lord God most high.
5. *El Shaddai* — the Almighty God.
6. *Jehovah-Jireh* — God, our Provider.
7. *Jehovah-Repheka* — God, our Healer.
8. *Jehovah-Tsidkenu* — God, our Righteousness.
9. *Jehovah-Nissi* — God, the Conqueror.
10. *Jehovah-Shalom* — God, our Peace.
11. *Jehovah-Shammah* — the God who is *there.*
12. *Jehovah-m'Kaddesh* — the Lord who sanctifies.
13. *Jehovah-Ro'eh* — God, our Shepherd.
14. *Jehovah-Olam* — God, the everlasting One.

These Hebrew names for God reveal *who He is to us.* In hallowing His names in prayer we are expressing faith to the Father. We see Him in all His power. He *will provide.* He *will heal.* He *is my Shepherd;* He *will guide me.* He has *imparted His peace, His righteousness and*

His sanctification to me. He is *my Conqueror* who has defeated the enemy. He is always *there.*

God sent His Son, Jesus, to be the fulfillment of everything His names represent. The name of Jesus is to be hallowed in the same way that we sanctify the names of the Father. "Wherefore God also hath highly exalted him, and given him a name which is above every name: That at the name of Jesus every knee should bow, of things in heaven, and things in earth, and things under the earth; And that every tongue should confess that Jesus Christ is Lord, to the glory of God the Father" (Phil. 2:9-11).

Jesus said, "Hitherto have ye asked nothing in my name: ask, and ye shall receive, that your joy may be full" (John 16:24). As we comprehend the power inherent in the name of our Lord we are able to appropriate the promises of God as we pray.

III. *Thy kingdom come.* This line from the Lord's Prayer is extremely significant because it is a petition in which we are asking for God's rule in our lives. Jesus emphasized the importance of this petition in the Sermon on the Mount: "But seek ye first *the kingdom of God,* and his righteousness; and all these things shall be added unto you" (Matt. 6:33).

When Jesus truly becomes the Lord of our lives, we no longer have to worry about anything. A king takes care of his subjects. He directs their lives. He supplies their needs. The king is responsible for everything that happens in his domain. He provides protection and oversees the details of life in his kingdom. In the same way, our Lord supplies these needs to us as we allow His kingdom to come in our lives. In His authority we find our peace.

Through prayer, we present ourselves before our Sovereign's throne. We petition Him to intervene in our lives, to help us with our problems. Because He is our

King, we are able to approach Him with confidence, in the full realization that He will hear us and He will undertake in our behalf. "Let us therefore come boldly unto the throne of grace, that we may obtain mercy, and find grace to help in time of need" (Heb. 4:16).

IV. *Thy will be done in earth, as it is in heaven.* We have already established that God is our heavenly Father who loves us with an everlasting love. He wants to have a relationship with us and He wants to bless us. This is His will.

His names give us further insights into His will for us. He wants us to have peace, to experience His righteousness, to know His power, to receive His guidance, to worship Him, to receive healing and to recognize His providence in our lives.

We have also reflected on the Lordship of Jesus Christ. He is our King. Because these things are true, it is imperative for us to get in tune with God's will. When we know His will, we are able to obey Him. The Bible says, "Now we know that God heareth not sinners: but if any man be a worshipper of God, *and doeth his will,* him he heareth" (John 9:31).

In asking for the Father's will to be done in earth, therefore, we are beseeching God to reveal His will to us so that we will be able to obey Him in all things. It is through our obedience that His will can be accomplished in earth.

Obedience to the will of the Father is an absolute prerequisite to answered prayer. God is love (see 1 John 4), and His Father's heart is filled with love for His children. He wants His children to express their love for Him in prayer and by obedience to His will. "If ye love me, keep my commandments" (John 14:15).

The commandments are found in the Word of God. The power to keep the commandments is found in the Holy Spirit. Paul wrote, "That the righteousness of the law might be fulfilled in us, who walk not after the flesh, but after the Spirit" (Rom. 8:4). When we pray the promises of God in the power of the Holy Spirit we are praying in the will of God. "And this is the confidence that we have in him, that, if we ask any thing according to his will, he heareth us; And if we know that he hear us, whatsoever we ask, we know that we have the petitions that we desired of him" (1 John 5:14,15).

V. *Give us this day our daily bread.* In this general request, our Lord is showing us that we need to bring our *specific needs* to the Father in prayer on a *daily basis.* We can pray for spiritual, emotional, physical, financial and social needs in the full expectation that He will meet those needs. Paul wrote, "But my God shall supply all your need according to his riches in glory by Christ Jesus" (Phil 4:19). What a wonderful promise this is.

It is significant to note where Jesus placed this phrase in His model prayer. Before we can ask the Father to meet our specific, daily needs with confidence, we need to be sure that we know Him as our Father and Lord and that our lives are in tune with His will.

God wants to bless you, and He "is able to do exceeding abundantly above all that we ask or think, according to the power that worketh in us" (Eph. 3: 20). First, however, we need to be sure that our priorities are in order; that we are in fact seeking the Kingdom of God and His righteousness first in our lives. Then, and only then, will all these things (that we pray for) be added unto us.

VI. *And forgive us our debts as we forgive our debtors.* Through forgiveness we enter the very heart of God. He wants us to confess our sins to Him so He can cleanse us. "If we confess our sins, he is faithful and just to forgive us our sins, and to cleanse us from all unrighteousness" (1 John 1:9).

Sin separates us from God and from our fellow-believers. Confession restores those relationships and brings forgiveness. The Psalmist wrote, "If I regard iniquity in my heart, the Lord will not hear me" (Ps. 66:18). Sin needs to be dealt with if we want God to hear our prayers.

The model prayer of Jesus asks God to forgive us in the same way we forgive others. What a sobering thought! Do I really want God to forgive me in the same way I forgive others? We must not minimize the importance of forgiving others when they wrong us.

Peter went to Jesus with a question, "Lord, how oft shall my brother sin against me, and I forgive him? Till seven times?" (Matt. 18:21).

"I say not unto thee, Until seven times," Jesus replied, "But, until seventy times seven" (Matt. 18:22).

The principle we need to consider here is: we must forgive others as often as we want to be forgiven. "If a man say, I love God, and hateth his brother, he is a liar: for he that loveth not his brother whom he hath seen, how can he love God whom he hath not seen?" (1 John 4:20).

Love is the greatest commandment of all. It takes no account of a wrong suffered (See 1 Corinthians 13). Through love we are able to forgive and maintain a proper attitude toward others. As we are motivated by love in our prayers, God (who is love) hears us, forgives us and answers us. As Paul states in Galatians 5:6, "the only thing that counts is faith expressing itself through love."

VII. *And lead us not into temptation.* We are engaged in a spiritual warfare. No one knew the impact of this warfare better than our Lord Jesus who "was led by the Spirit into the wilderness. Being forty days tempted of the devil" (Luke 4:1, 2). Tempted in all points as we are, He remained sinless (See Hebrews 4:15). In Him who overcame the world we can be strong. "Finally, my brethren, be strong in the Lord, and in the power of his might. Put on the whole armour of God, that ye may be able to stand against the wiles of the devil" (Eph. 6:10, 11).

Every morning, after we've acknowledged the glory of the Father and the Lordship of Jesus Christ, and we've examined our lives to be certain we're in the will of the Lord, and that we are in right relationship with Him and others, we need to get dressed and equipped for our walk in the world where we will encounter temptations from the adversary. Put on every piece of God's armor every day. Gird your loins with truth. Protect your heart and chest with the breastplate of His righteousness. Cover your feet with the gospel of peace. Use the shield of faith to quench all the fiery darts of the wicked one. Wear the helmet of salvation to protect your head and mind, and take the sword of the Spirit (the Word of God) to slay the enemy. (See Ephesians 6:10-18)

By clothing himself with the armor of God, our Lord defeated the enemy in His life. In the wilderness He rebuked Satan as follows: "It is written, That man shall not live by bread alone, but by every word of God" (Luke 4:4). Jesus defeated Satan with the Word of God.

God's armor is not complete, however, unless it is put on with prayer. Paul wrote, "Praying always with all prayer and supplication in the Spirit, and watching thereunto with all perseverance and supplication for all saints" (Eph.6:18). Put on each piece of God's armor prayerfully, remembering to intercede for others who are engaged in battle also.

VIII. *Deliver us from evil.* After we have engaged in spiritual warfare successfully, as God has outlined in His Word, we can be assured of His deliverance. Paul wrote, "There hath no temptation taken you but such as is common to man: but God is faithful, who will not suffer you to be tempted above that ye are able; but will with the temptation also make a way to escape, that ye may be able to bear it" (1 Cor. 10:13).

God will make a way for you to escape. He is your Deliverer. It is He who enables us to stand in the evil day. He has promised to place a hedge of protection around us as we follow His ways.

"The fear of man bringeth a snare: but whoso putteth his trust in the Lord shall be safe" (Prov. 29:25).

IX. *For thine is the kingdom, and the power, and the glory, for ever.* How appropriate it is for our Lord to conclude His model prayer by praising and honoring God for who He is and for all He has done. Jesus is showing us the importance of thanksgiving and praise in our prayer life. "Know ye that the Lord he is God: it is he that hath made us, and not we ourselves; we are his people and the sheep of his pasture. Enter into his gates with thanksgiving, and into his courts with praise: be thankful unto him, and bless his name. For the Lord is good; his mercy is everlasting; and his truth endureth to all generations" (Ps. 100:3-5).

Interestingly, the conclusion of the Lord's Prayer leads us through the gates of the Lord and into His courts. It speaks of our need to live in His presence continually.

Brother Lawrence wrote, "All we have to do is to recognize God as being intimately present within us. Then we may speak directly to Him every time we need to ask for help, to know His will in moments of uncertainty, and to do whatever He wants us to do in a way that pleases

Him. We should offer our works to Him before we begin, and thank Him afterwards for the privilege of having done them for His sake. This continuous conversation would also include praising and loving God incessantly for His infinite goodness and perfection." (From *The Practice of the Presence of God* by Brother Lawrence.)

The Lord's Prayer is even more than the model prayer of Jesus. It is also an introduction to an entirely new way of looking at things — an exciting life style — a life totally enveloped by and clothed with the presence of the Lord. Such a life is rooted and grounded in prayer.

The nine principles of prayer from the model prayer of Jesus form a framework on which to build personal prayers that appropriate God's promises and incorporate them into your life. With this in mind, we have developed a personal prayer that you can use as you start to pray in the way Jesus showed us. This personal prayer incorporates the words of Scripture. As the remainder of this book reveals, praying the Word of God is effective because it releases faith in the believer's heart and it coincides with the will of God. God promises that His Word will not return unto Him void. Fill in your specific requests as you use this prayer that is based on the example of our Lord. "*After this manner* therefore pray ye..." (Matt. 6:9).

PERSONAL PRAYER FROM THE
MODEL PRAYER OF JESUS:

Heavenly Father, I thank you that you have given me the power to become your child. I trust you, Father, and I desire to become like a little child in your presence for I realize that whosoever does not receive your kingdom like a little child shall in no wise enter into it. I thank you that I have not received the spirit of bondage again to fear; but you have given me the Spirit of adoption, whereby I am able to cry, "Abba, Father." Father, I adore you.

It is such a privilege to be a part of your family, Father. Thank you for the great love with which you love me and accept me into the family of your beloved. Thank you for taking good care of me. Thank you for your faithfulness.

Your wonderful names declare your marvelous promises to me, Father. You are Almighty God and you never change. You are the Father of lights with whom there is no variableness nor shadow of turning. You are the Giver of every good and perfect gift. You are the same yesterday, today and forever. You are the eternal God of the universe and you have given me eternal life. Only you are worthy of worship because you are the majestic Ruler of all your marvelous creation. You are the God most high. All power in heaven and in earth is yours. You are my healer, the Great Physician, and by your stripes I am healed — made whole in every respect. You are my Provider, the Source of all my supply. You shower blessings upon me from your storehouse. You are always more than enough, the God of abundant life. You are my righteousness. All my righteousness is as filthy rags, Lord, but through your righteousness I am washed clean. You have conquered the enemy in my life, Lord, and he no longer has access to me because of your shed blood on Calvary. You are my peace, and how I praise you that as I bring my petitions before you in faith and thanksgiving, you minister your peace which passes understanding. There is no longer any guilt or worry in my life because you are my peace. Thank you for being there whenever I need you, Lord, a very present help in time of trouble. You have sanctified me by setting me apart for your service and you are guiding me. You are my Good Shepherd and I shall never want for any good thing. Thank you, Father, that you are the everlasting One, the eternal I AM, the first and the last. You are everything to me.

I crown you, Lord Jesus, as the King of kings and Lord of lords in my life. I submit my life to you by denying myself, taking up my cross and following you. I put you first in my life and give you complete control of all I am and have. I will dwell in your kingdom, where there is righteousness, joy, peace and love in the Holy Spirit, forevermore. Halleujah!

I delight to do your will, O Lord. I will study Your Word and learn Your ways. Give me the grace to obey your commandments and to follow you with all my heart. Thank you for revealing your will to me. I will obey you, Lord, as you unfold your will to me. May your will be done in me and in all the earth as it is in heaven. Keep me in the center of your will.

You have promised to supply my daily needs, Father. How I thank you for your faithfulness in my life. You will never let me down. I present my needs to you now, Lord, because I know you want to bless me and I realize you are the Source of all I have or ever will have. Give me this day the following needs of my life: _____

_____

_____ .

Thank you, Father. Please forgive me for those things in which I have failed you. I now bring my specific sins before you, confessing them in the Name of Jesus Christ, my Lord, who is the one mediator between me and you. I confess the following sins: _____

_____ .

Thank you for the wonderful gift of repentance that prepares the way for you to move in my life. Thank you for the wonderful blessing of forgiveness. I now consciously accept your wonderful cleansing and refreshing. Sin no longer has dominion over me. There is therefore now no condemnation to me as I continue to walk in your Spirit.

I am pure, holy and blameless before you, in love. Thank you for setting me free. Laying aside every weight, and the sin that so easily besets me, I run with patience the race that is set before me, looking unto you, Lord Jesus, the Author and Finisher of my faith.

As I continue in prayer, Lord, I realize that there are those who have something against me. Reveal to me every relationship in my life where problems exist between me and another. Father, through the power of your Spirit, I willingly forgive _____ for the wrongs they have committed against me. As you direct me, I will go to _____ to seek forgiveness for the things I've done to wrong him/her/them. Thank you for the cleansing power of forgiveness. Keep me sensitive to your voice. Give me a pure heart, Father.

I know you will never lead me into temptation, Lord. I will prepare myself for the spiritual warfare that rages in our world today. I put on the whole armor you have provided for me. I gird my loins with your truth. On my chest I am wearing the breastplate of your righteousness. The gospel of peace covers my feet. I strap the shield of faith to my forearm so I will be able to quench all the enemy's fiery darts. The helmet of your salvation protects my mind from all assaults. Thank you for the powerful weapon of your Word — the sword of the Spirit — with which I can take the offensive in the warfare against Satan and all the forces of evil. I will stand in the evil day, praying with all prayer and supplication through your Spirit, Lord. I will persevere in prayer, interceding for all saints.

I thank you for delivering me from evil, Lord. I do not need to fear anything or anyone, for you are my light and my salvation and you are always with me. You will never leave me nor forsake me. You are a mighty buckler to all those who trust in you. You will light my candle; you will enlighten my darkness. By your strength, Lord,

I can and will run through a troop and I have leaped over a wall. Your way is perfect; your Word is tried. You gird me with strength and you make my way perfect. You teach my hands to war. You have girded me with strength unto the battle and you have delivered me. Halleujah!

Yours is the kingdom and the power and the glory forever. I love you, Lord. I rejoice in you. How I thank you for all you have done in and through my life. It is a good thing to give thanks unto you, O Lord. I sing praises to your name, O Most High. I rejoice in your lovingkindness and your tender mercies. O Lord, you have made me glad through your work. You reign, O King! You are clothed with majesty and with strength. Your throne is established forever. I will praise you with my whole heart. Your works are honorable and glorious and your righteousness endures forever. Thank you for being my Father and my Lord. Thank you for giving me my daily bread. Thank you for delivering me from evil. Thank you for forgiving me. O Lord, my God, I will thank you and praise you forevermore!

PRAYERS THAT PREVAIL

PART I
Prayers for the Christian Walk

A. Walking with Jesus

B. Spiritual Power

C. Fruitfulness

D. The Inner Life

WALKING WITH JESUS

1

Receiving Jesus As Savior and Lord

Key Thought: Salvation is free because Jesus paid for it.

Key Scripture: *"For God so loved the world, that he gave his only begotten Son, that whosoever believeth in him should not perish, but have everlasting life" (John 3:16).*

Prayer: Father in heaven, thank you for sending your Son, Jesus, to die on the cross for me, and for His blood that was shed to redeem me[1] and to cleanse me from my sins.[2] Father, you commended your love toward me, in that, while I was yet a sinner, Jesus died for me.[3] It is true that I have sinned against you in many ways and fallen far short of your glory.[4] The just wages of sin is death, but I don't want that death, Father. Instead, I want the gift of eternal life in Christ Jesus.[5]

Lord, I am sorry and I repent of my sins.[6] Forgive me.[7] By repentance I understand that I must change the course of my life. I now turn and go in the opposite direction from the way of sin and I determine in my heart to follow you, no matter what the cost may be.

I invite you to become the Lord of my life from this point forward, forever. Jesus, I now receive you as my Savior and Lord. I openly proclaim and confess that you are the Lord of my life. I believe in my heart that you have been raised from the dead. Therefore I am saved.[8] I now belong to you. I believe that you have cleansed me from all sin by your precious blood.[2] I am now in Christ. I am a new creature. The old things have passed away. All things have become new.[9] I am a child of God.[10]

What shall I render unto you, Lord, for all your benefits toward me? I will take the cup of salvation and call upon your matchless name throughout all my days.[11] You, Lord Jesus, are able to save to the uttermost all who come to God through you.[12] You have now become the way, the truth and the life to me.[13] I will trust in you and not be afraid. You are my strength and my song; you have become my salvation.[14] Thank you, Jesus, for giving yourself for me and for redeeming me from all iniquity.[15] Thank you for loving me and setting me free. Thank you for choosing me from the beginning to receive salvation through the sanctification of your Spirit and belief of the truth.[16]

References: (1)*Ephesians 1:7* (2)*1 John 1:7* (3)*Romans 5:8* (4)*Romans 3:23* (5)*Romans 6:23* (6)*2 Corinthians 7:10* (7)*1 John 1:9* (8)*Romans 10:9,10* (9)*2 Corinthians 5:17* (10)*John 1:12* (11)*Psalms 116:12,13* (12)*Hebrews 7:25* (13)*John 14:6* (14)*Isaiah 12:2* (15)*Titus 2:11,14* (16)*2 Thessalonians 2:13.*

2

Abiding in Christ

Key Thought: Abiding in Jesus leads to fruitfulness.

Key Scripture: *"Abide in me, and I in you. As the branch cannot bear fruit of itself, except it abide in the vine; no more can ye, except ye abide in me. I am the vine, ye are the branches: He that abideth in me, and I in him, the same bringeth forth much fruit: for without me ye can do nothing"* (John 15:4-5).

Prayer: Lord Jesus, I want to abide in you constantly. I know that if I abide in you, and your words abide in me, I may ask what I will and it will be accomplished.[1] Abiding in you, Lord, will keep me from sin[2] and make me fruitful in your kingdom.[3] So many important things stem from abiding in you. Teach me to abide — to settle, dwell, take root — in you.

You, Lord, are the vine. I am but a branch whose life stems from you. Thank you for grafting me into your vine and for pruning me of all the things in my life that do not lead to growth and fruitfulness.[4]

I now understand that I can accomplish nothing apart from you,[3] but through you I can do *all things*.[5]

I will endeavor to obey your command to love others.[6] I realize this is possible only insofar as I abide in you and you in me.[7]

Lord, you are my refuge and my fortress: my God, in you will I trust as I abide under your shadow and dwell in the secret place of your presence.[8] Thank you for sending your Holy Spirit to abide with me forever,[9] and for showing me the secret of abiding in the Father's love.[10]

It brings me great joy to know that you have bought me with a price, and that it is my responsibility to serve you first, before others.[11] Thank you for calling me.

You have imparted to me the anointing of your Holy Spirit which now abides within me and teaches me as I abide in you. Because of your abiding presence I now have confidence and will have no reason to be ashamed at your coming.[12]

References: (1)John 15:7 (2)1 John 3:6 (3)John 15:5
(4)John 15:1,2 (5)Philippians 4:13 (6)John 15:12 (7)John 15:10
(8)Psalms 91:1 (9)John 14:16 (10)1 John 3:24
(11)1 Corinthians 7:23 (12)1 John 2:27,28

3

Growing in Christ

Key Thought: Daily renewal through the Word of God leads to growth.

Key Scripture: *"And he shall be like a tree planted by the rivers of water, that bringeth forth his fruit in his season; his leaf also shall not wither; and whatsoever he doeth shall prosper"* *(Ps. 1:3).*

Prayer: Thank you, Lord, for showing me that growth is a part of all life. It is necessary for survival and health. I want to grow in you, to become all that you have planned for me to be.

Help me to remember that my conversion experience was only the beginning of my new life with you. Father, you are helping me to grow in the Lord Jesus.

Thank you that in the inward man I am being renewed day by day[1] — that you are perfecting the things that concern me[2] — that I am being renewed in knowledge after the image of my Creator.[3]

Your wonderful work continues in my life, and I always want to follow you. Thank you for nurturing me and leading me each step of the way.

Laying aside all malice, guile, hypocrisy, envy and evil speaking, I desire the pure milk of the Word of God that I might grow thereby.[4] I want to grow in you, Lord; feed me from your Word — the Bread of Life.[5]

You are building your church upon the foundation of the apostles and prophets. You, Lord Jesus, are the chief cornerstone; in whom all the building fitly framed together grows unto an holy temple.[6] Thank you for letting me be one of your "living stones," and for letting me grow within your body.[7]

Grant that I will never be childish, tossed to and fro, and carried about with every wind of doctrine, by the sleight of men, and cunning craftiness, but speaking the truth in love, I want to grow up into you in all things. Forgive me for the times when I have been childish and have been so easily influenced by others. Forgive me for the times when I know I should have spoken the truth in love, but failed to do so.[8]

When I was a child, I spoke as a child, I understood as a child, I thought as a child; but now that I am an adult, I must put away childish things.[9] You have made all things new to me[10] and you are helping me to grow up in you. I choose to put away all childish things from my life, and to replace them with godly things that reflect and produce spiritual maturity.

You are helping me, Father, to grow in grace, and in the knowledge of my Lord and Savior Jesus Christ. To Him be glory![11] Amen.

As I behold your glory, Lord, you change me into your image from glory to glory, even as by the Spirit.[12] Thank you for Christian growth that develops qualities within me that will help my life to conform to your image. It is exciting to realize that this is your goal for my life.

References: (1)2 Corinthians 4:16 (2)Psalms 138:8 (3)Colossians 3:10 (4)1 Peter 2:2 (5)John 6:35 (6)Ephesians 2:20,21 (7)1 Peter 2:5 (8)Ephesians 4:15 (9)1 Corinthians 13:11 (10)2 Corinthians 5:17 (11)2 Peter 3:18 (12)2 Corinthians 3:18 Other Scriptures: Psalms 1

4
Walking in Obedience

Key Thought: "Obedience means marching right on whether we feel like it or not" (Dwight L. Moody).

Key Scripture: *"Behold, I set before you this day a blessing and a curse; A blessing, if ye obey the commandments of the Lord your God, which I command you this day: And a curse, if ye will not obey the commandments of the Lord your God, but turn aside out of the way which I command you this day, to go after other gods, which ye have not known" (Deut. 11:26-28).*

Prayer: Heavenly Father, teach me to obey all your commandments. It is true that obeying your voice is far better than any sacrifice because rebellion is as the sin of witchcraft in your sight, Lord, and stubbornness is as iniquity and idolatry.[1] May I never be found guilty of those sins.

Please forgive me, Father, for each time when I have rebelled against you. I repent of all my acts of disobedience and my failure to do what you have commanded. Henceforth, I want to obey you in everything.

Thank you for opening my ears to discipline. Lord, you have commanded me to turn from iniquity and have promised that if I will obey and serve you, I will spend my days in prosperity and my years in pleasures,[2] and it will be well with me.[3]

Help me to see that obeying you leads to so many good things. You have promised to give the Holy Spirit to all who obey you, Lord. Please fill me with your Spirit as I walk in obedience to you. I want to obey you with joy, out of the sense of delight that follows whenever I do your will.[4]

Thank you for all the promises of your Word, Lord, which will come to pass in my life as I learn to obey you. You have pointed out that if I love you I will obey you.[5] I do love you, Lord, and I want to obey you from my heart. Even the winds and sea obey you, Lord.[6] I know it is my responsibility to obey you rather than men.

I know it is faith that enables me to do so. Help me, Lord, to be like Abraham, who obeyed in faith, nothing wavering, and went out, not knowing where he was going, but believing in you to lead him.[7] Through obedience and faith I enter your glorious rest.

Thank you for your promise, Lord, that as I express my love for you and obey your commandments and keep your words, I am loved by you and the Father and you both will love me and come to me and make your home with me.[8]

Thank you for leading me into a life of obedience.

References: (1)*1 Samuel 15:22,23* (2)*Job 36:10,11*
(3)*Ephesians 6:1-3* (4)*Psalms 40:8* (5)*John 14:15* (6)*Psalms 65:7*
(7)*Hebrews 11:8* (8)*John 14:21,23* **Other Scriptures:** *Psalms 18:44,*
Jeremiah 7:23, Jeremiah 26:13, Jeremiah 42:6, Zechariah 6:15,
Matthew 8:27, Acts 5:29-32, Romans 6:17

5

Who the Lord Is to Me

Key Thought: Jesus is everything to me.

Key Scripture: *"Jesus saith unto him, I am the way, the truth, and the life: no man cometh unto the Father but by me" (John 14:6).*

Prayer: Lord Jesus, you are my Shepherd; I shall not want. You lead me.[1] You are the Good Shepherd[2] and we are the sheep of your pasture.[3] Thank you for your tender care.

You are the door that opens to an entirely new life.[4] You are my fortress, my sure defense.[5] You are the rock upon whom the Church is built and the gates of hell will never prevail against it.[6] You make me feel secure.

You are my peace, my hope, my health, my all. The Rock of refuge, my high tower, my shield and buckler.[7] You protect me, Lord. You keep me safe.

You are the Word that became flesh and dwelt among us[8] — the Word of Life.[9] You are Immanuel — God with us.[10] And you are my righteousness and the strength of my life. You are my light and my salvation, of what should I be afraid?[11] Thank you for always being with me, Lord.

I thank you that you are the first and the last, the Alpha and Omega.[12] You are the Sun of righteousness,[13] the fragrant Rose of Sharon and the fairest of ten thousand. You are the Lily of the Valley[14] — the bright and morning star.[15] You are the light of the world, and in you there is no darkness at all.[16] Help me walk in your light at all times, Lord.

You are called Wonderful, Counselor, the Mighty God, the everlasting Father and the Prince of Peace.[17] You are the Holy One of Israel, the Lamb that was slain from the foundation of the world.[18]

You are Jesus, the Savior of the world, and yet you are my personal Lord and Savior and friend. I stand in awe and reverence of your matchless gift of love for me, for, even though you are the King of kings and Lord of lords, you willingly died for *me*.

At your name, every knee must bow and every tongue must confess that you are Lord to the glory of God the Father,[19] yet you are the God in whom I live and move and have my being[20] in whom all my needs are met.[21]

Exalt your name in all the earth, Lord, so that others will see that you are the only thing in life that really matters.

References: (1)*Psalms 23* (2)*John 10:14* (3)*Psalms 100:3*
(4)*John 10:9-11* (5)*Psalms 89:18* (6)*Matthew 16:18* (7)*Psalms 18:30*
(8)*John 1:14* (9)*1 John 1:1* (10)*Isaiah 7:14* (11)*Psalms 27:1*
(12)*Revelation 1 :8* (13)*Malachi 4:2* (14)*Song of Solomon 2:1*
(15)*Revelation 22:16* (16)*1 John 1:5* (17)*Isaiah 9:6*
(18)*Revelation 13:8* (19)*Philippians 2:10* (20)*Acts 17:28*
(21)*Philippians 4:19* **Other Scriptures:** *Psalms 31:1*

SPIRITUAL POWER

6

Being Filled With the Holy Spirit

Key Thought: Unless the Holy Spirit fills, the human spirit fails.

Key Scripture: *"Be filled with the Spirit; Speaking to yourselves in psalms and hymns and spiritual songs, singing and making melody in your heart to the Lord; Giving thanks always for all things unto God and the Father in the name of our Lord Jesus Christ" (Eph. 5:18-20).*

Prayer: Heavenly Father, thank you for sending the Holy Spirit to be with us forever. He is the Paraclete, the divine Comforter, the Spirit of truth.[1] Thank you for your promise to give the Holy Spirit to those who ask you.[2] Fill me with your Spirit, Lord, as I wait before you.[3]

I receive your Holy Spirit now, Lord, and I want to live in such a way that I would never grieve Him.[4] Because the same Spirit that raised Christ from the dead dwells in me, I have newness of life. Thank you for the convicting and transforming power of your Spirit, Lord. What a miracle it is to realize that the Spirit of my Lord Jesus Christ dwells in me![5]

Because your Spirit dwells within me, Lord, I am able to be led by Him just as Jesus was led by the Spirit into the wilderness to be tempted of the devil.[6] Help me to follow the leading of your Holy Spirit, for as many as are led by the Spirit are your sons, Lord.[7]

You promised that you would not leave us comfortless,[8] so you sent your Spirit to fill us and guide us.[9] Help me to see what that really means. You, Lord Jesus, possess all power in heaven and earth, and you have promised to empower me with your Spirit. Because you have gone to be with your Father, I am able to accomplish the things you desire, for your life and power dwell within me by your Spirit.[10]

Your Spirit gives me power to be your witness and to speak your Word with boldness.

Being filled with your Spirit, Lord, I will give myself continually to prayer and your Word. Help me to remember that the infilling of the Holy Spirit brings wisdom and faith, and help me to draw upon the power of your Spirit each day of my life.

References: *(1)John 14:16 (2)Luke 11:13 (3)Acts 13:52 (4)Ephesians 4:30 (5)Romans 8:11 (6)Luke 4:1 (7)Romans 8:14 (8)John 14:18 (9)John 16:13 (10)John 14:12* **Other Scriptures:** *Luke 1:15, Acts 2:4, Acts 4:31, Acts 9:17, Acts 19:2,6, 2 Timothy 1:14*

7

Walking in the Spirit

Key Thought: It's an adventure to be led by the Spirit of God.

Key Scripture: *"There is therefore now no condemnation to them which are in Christ Jesus, who walk not after the flesh, but after the Spirit. For the law of the Spirit of life in Christ Jesus hath made me free from the law of sin and death" (Rom. 8:1-2).*

Prayer: Thank you, Lord, for filling me with your Spirit. Help me to endeavor always to walk in the Spirit and not in the flesh. You are pouring out your Spirit upon all flesh, Jesus, and there is such power in Him.[1] I want always to walk in your Spirit for the rest of my days. Where you lead me, Lord, I *will* follow.[2]

Your grace enables me to walk in your Spirit, Lord, and your grace and power alone preserve me from walking in the flesh.[3] Help me to yield more and more to the power of your Spirit. Because I am led by your Spirit, I am not under the law of sin and death.[4]

I choose to crucify my flesh, Lord, with all its affections and lusts so that I may live in the Spirit and walk in the Spirit.[5] The carnal mind is enmity against you, Lord, and it is impossible to please you in the flesh. Because your Spirit dwells within me, however, it is now possible for me to walk in the Spirit.[6] Praise your name.

As many as are led by your Spirit are the sons of God.[7] Thank you for granting me that privilege, Lord, and for giving me the Spirit of adoption, whereby I am able to cry, "Abba, Father."[8] As your son/daughter I will always strive to please you. Thank you for showing me your will through your Word, and for giving me the power to obey you.

As I walk in your mighty Spirit, Lord, signs and wonders will follow my preaching of your gospel. And the indwelling Holy Spirit in my life makes me your temple.[9] What an honor all that is, Lord. May I never misrepresent your gospel or defile your temple in any way. I never want to dishonor you, Lord.

Thank you for the fruit of your Spirit in my life.[10] May others taste of your fruit and hunger after you. The fruit of the Spirit in my life leads me into all goodness and righteousness and truth.[11] Thank you, Lord.

Thank you for all the promises you fulfill in my life as I choose to walk in your Spirit, Lord. I receive your promises by faith as I press forward in your Spirit toward the mark for the prize of your high calling.[12]

References: *(1)Joel 2:28 (2)Luke 9:57-62 (3)Galatians 5:16,17 (4)Romans 8:1,2 (5)Galatians 5:25 (6)Romans 8:9 (7)Romans 8:14 (8)Galatians 4:6 (9)1 Corinthians 3:16 (10)Galatians 5:22-25 (11)Ephesians 5:9 (12)Philippians 3:13,14* **Other Scriptures:** *Romans 8:26, Romans 15:19, 1 Peter 1:11*

8
Walking in Victory

Key Thought: Thanks be to God who gives me victory in every area of my life.

Key Scripture: *"He will swallow up death in victory; and the Lord God will wipe away tears from off all faces; and the rebuke of his people shall he take away from off all the earth: for the Lord hath spoken it"* (Isa. 25:8).

Prayer: Thank you, Lord, for victory. Jesus' death on the cross and His resurrection from the dead assure me of victory in this life and the life to come. Death no longer has any sting; the grave has no victory. Thanks be to God who gives me the victory through my Lord Jesus Christ![1]

The accuser of the brethren seeks to defeat me, but you have already defeated him. I have victory over him through your blood, and by the word of my testimony.[2]

Thank you, Father, for victory over every weakness and problem in my life. I will live and walk in the victory Jesus bought for me at so great a price. Forgive me, Lord, for the times when I've allowed circumstances and doubts to defeat me. I will always remember that it is faith that gives me the victory to overcome the world. Because I have been born of you, Lord, I can claim your victory over the world.[3]

Because of the victory you purchased for me, Lord, I will be steadfast, unmoveable, always abounding in your work. I know that my labor will not be in vain because your victory upholds my life.[1] You have given me victory over every sin and temptation. Hallelujah!

Yours, O Lord, is the greatness, and the power, and the glory, and the victory, and the majesty: for all that is in heaven and in the earth is yours. Yours is the kingdom, O Lord, and you are exalted as head above all. Both riches and honor come from you, and you reign over all; and in your hand is power and might; and in your hand it is to make great, and to give strength unto all.[4] Now, therefore, my God, I thank you, and I praise your glorious name. I receive your strength and victory into my life. Your victory makes me a winner!

I sing unto you, Lord, a new song; for you have done marvelous things: your right hand, and your holy arm have already gotten me the victory in all the areas of struggle in my life. Praise you, Lord![5]

Because of your victory I rejoice and live secure in the knowledge that nothing shall be able to separate me from your love, Lord Jesus, my victory.[6]

References: (1)1 Corinthians 15:55-58 (2)Revelation 12:10-12 (3)1 John 5:4,5 (4)1 Chronicles 29:11-13 (5)Psalms 98:1 (6)Romans 8:38,39 Other Scriptures: John 16:33, Romans 3:4, Romans 12:21, 1 John 2:13, 1 John 4:4

9

Walking in Faith

Key Thought: Faith comes through hearing God's Word.

Key Scripture: *"Now faith is the substance of things hoped for, the evidence of things not seen...without faith it is impossible to please him: for he that cometh to God must believe that he is, and that he is a rewarder of them that diligently seek him" (Heb. 11:1,6).*

Prayer: Your Word, O Lord, unlocks the doors of faith for me to enter. Walking in faith is an exciting life style, full of adventure and peace. Thank you for your gift of faith in my life.

Increase my faith, Lord. When I pray for wisdom or any other thing, let me remember to ask in faith, nothing wavering. I realize, Lord, that he who wavers is like a wave of the sea driven with the wind and tossed.[1]

Help me to remember that when my faith wavers, I cannot receive from you. But I am not one who cannot receive, I am a believer, not a doubter. When doubt comes, I cast it away because it exalts itself against God.[2] But I will believe you, Lord, and not doubt. O Lord, I believe your Word. Help me root it out when unbelief tries to creep into my heart. Keep me, Lord, from becoming double-minded. I choose to be single-minded, walking in faith, with my eyes fixed on you.

Help me to remember that the just shall live by your faith.[3] May I always have faith to move mountains, to realize that nothing is impossible to one who has faith.[4] I look to Stephen's example, Lord; a man full of faith and power, doing great wonders in your name.[5]

Thank you for showing me that whatsoever is not of faith is sin.[6] Let me see the wonderful relationship that exists between faith, holiness and happiness. Bless me, Father, as I follow the course of faith.

It is my desire, Lord, to continue in your faith, grounded and settled, and to not be moved away from the hope of the gospel.[7] Keep me steadfast in my faith, Lord, walking in Christ and rooted and built up in Him. Establish me in the faith; let me always abound in thanksgiving for your great gifts to me. You have revealed yourself to me in so many ways — through your Word, your Spirit, and the changes you've wrought in my life. I believe in you with all my heart and I will walk in faith each day, for faith is the victory that overcomes the world.[8]

Help me express my faith through love for that demonstrates that my faith is real.[9]

When trials come, Lord, I know my faith in you will see me through. It is wonderful to realize that the trial of faith is much more precious than of gold that perishes, though it be tried by fire.[10] May I be enabled by your grace to withstand the trials of life in such a way that my faith will be found unto praise and honor and glory at the appearing of my Lord Jesus Christ.

References: (1)James 1:5-8, (2)2 Corinthians 10:5 (3)Habakkuk 2:4 (4)Matthew 17:20 (5)Acts 6:8 (6)Romans 14:22,23 (7)Colossians 1:23 (8)1 John 5:4 (9)Galatians 5:6 (10)1 Peter 1:7 Other Scriptures: Romans 10:17, 2 Thessalonians 1:3

10

Putting God First

Key Thought: God deserves first place in our lives.

Key Scripture: *"But seek ye first the kingdom of God, and his righteousness; and all these things shall be added unto you" (Matt. 6:33).*

Prayer: Lord, thank you for promising so many wonderful blessings to all who put you first. I want you to be first in my life at all times, Lord, and as I seek first your kingdom and righteousness, I trust you to supply all my need.

Your Word declares that my heart will be found where my treasure is. Lord, I want you to be my treasure.[1] You are the one God, the Father of all. You are above all and through all and in all believers.[2] Help me, Father, to keep you first and to keep all my priorities in line with yours.

You are the first and the last, O God. Beside you, there is no god.[3] All other objects of human worship are idols. May I never be guilty of idolatry, Lord.

Forgive me for each time when I have allowed other things in my life to take your place. I repent of any and all idolatry. I put you first in my life, Lord Jesus.[4]

Help me never to desire first place, Lord, because that position belongs only to you. Many that would be first shall be last; only those who put you first will be exalted.[5]

Lord Jesus, I ask you to show forth all longsuffering in my life, so that other people will see your marvelous plans and patterns and be drawn to believe on you unto life everlasting.[6] I crown you as the rightful King of my life. You are my Lord.

I love you, Lord, because you first loved me.[7] You are first in everything. You draw me and I run after you. Help me always to respond promptly to everything you initiate in my life.

Lord Jesus, you are the first and the last, and everything in between. You are alive forevermore.[8] God has given you a name that is above every name, that at your name, Lord Jesus, every knee should bow and every tongue confess that you are Lord, to the glory of God, the Father.[9] Praise your name, Lord.

References: (1)Matthew 6:21 (2)Ephesians 4:6 (3)Isaiah 44:6 (4)Exodus 20:3 (5)Matthew 19:30 (6)1 Timothy 1:16 (7)1 John 4:19 (8)Revelation 1:11,17 (9)Philippians 2:9-11 Other Scriptures: Matthew 6:33, Colossians 3:2

11
Walking in Strength

Key Thought: My weakness is God's opportunity to be strong.

Key Scripture: *"I can do all things through Christ which strengtheneth me" (Phil. 4:13).*

Prayer: Let the words of my mouth, and the meditation of my heart, be acceptable in your sight, O Lord, my strength and my Redeemer.[1] You are my light and my salvation; whom shall I fear? You are the strength of my life; of whom shall I be afraid?[2]

You are my strength and my shield, O Lord. You are my saving strength. When I walk in you, I walk in strength.[3] Your grace is all I need. Your wonderful strength is made perfect in my weakness.[4] When I am weak help me to remember to proclaim, "You, Lord, are strong!"[5]

Thank you for being there always to stand with me, Lord. You are always ready to strengthen me. You have granted to me, according to the riches of your glory, strength in my inner man by the might of your Spirit.[6] Hallelujah!

I receive your strength now to help me in my specific weakness(es): _____. Without you I can do nothing, but through you I can do all things. Lord Jesus, you are my strength.[1]

I have been strengthened with all might, according to your glorious power, unto all patience and longsuffering with joyfulness.[7] Because of the strength that you have imparted to me, Lord, I give thanks to you and I depend totally on you. You are the vine and I am the branch.[8]

You are the God of all grace, Father, and you have called me into your eternal glory. I can be confident even in suffering because I know you are at work in my life to make me perfect and to establish, strengthen and settle me.[9] Thank you, Lord.

Your strong arm has gotten me the victory in my area of weakness, Lord. You have done marvelous things for me — your right hand and your holy arm have delivered me.[10]

You are strengthening me according to your Word. You are making my feet like hinds' feet, so that I will be able to walk upon the high places.[11] I rejoice in you, Lord, and I joy in you for you are my salvation and my strength.

References: *(1)Psalms 19:14 (2)Psalms 27:1 (3)Psalms 28:8 (4)2 Corinthians 12:9 (5)Joel 3:10 (6)Ephesians 3:16 (7)Colossians 1:11 (8)John 15:5 (9)1 Peter 5:10 (10)Psalms 98:1 (11)Habakkuk 3:19* *Other Scriptures:* *Psalms 46:1, Psalms 89:10, Psalms 119:11, 2 Timothy 4:17*

12

Wearing God's Armor

Key Thought: Nothing can penetrate the strong armor of God.

Key Scripture: *"Finally, my brethren, be strong in the Lord, and in the power of his might. Put on the whole armour of God, that ye may be able to stand against the wiles of the devil" (Eph. 6:10-11).*

Prayer: Lord, I thank you for the armor you have provided for my protection. Help me to wear it daily and never to forget to put on a single piece of your protective gear. Each day, Lord, I will remember to put on the whole armor of God: to gird my loins with your truth and wear the breastplate of your righteousness; to shod my feet with the preparation of the gospel of peace and buckle the shield of faith to my forearm; to place on my head the helmet of salvation and take up the sword of the Spirit (the Word of God), praying with all supplication in the Spirit, and watching thereunto with all perseverance and supplication for all saints.[1]

Give me a clear sense concerning the spiritual warfare to which you've called me. I realize the cunning craftiness of the enemy, Lord,[2] and I desire to be prepared and equipped to stand against him in faith and power. Help me always to remember, Lord, that I am not wrestling against flesh and blood, but against principalities, powers, the rulers of the darkness of this world, and spiritual wickedness in high places.[3] For these reasons, I need to equip myself each day, Lord, with your armor. Thank you for fighting for me and protecting me.

I will be sober and vigilant, Lord, while wearing your armor, because my adversary, the devil, walks about as a roaring lion, seeking whom he may devour.[4] I resist him in the faith of your Word, Lord. I thank you that Satan is a defeated foe.

I thank you for your protection, Lord. I do not have to engage in spiritual warfare in the flesh, for the weapons of our warfare are not carnal, but mighty through God to the pulling down of strongholds. Through your power I will cast down imaginations, and every high thing that exalts itself against the knowledge of God, and I will bring every thought into captivity to obedience to you, Lord.[5]

Father, I will endure hardship as a good soldier and will not entangle myself with the affairs of this life, so that I may please you, who have armed me with your mighty armor and chosen me to be a soldier in your spiritual army. I gladly wear the whole armor you've given to me.

References: *(1)Ephesians 6:10-18 (2)Ephesians 4:14 (3)Ephesians 6:12 (4)1 Peter 5:8 (5)2 Corinthians 10:4* **Other Scriptures:** *2 Timothy 2:3,4, 1 John 4:4*

13

Capturing the Present Moment

Key Thought: The present moment is a precious gift.

Key Scripture: *"Forgetting those things which are behind, and reaching forth unto those things which are before, I press toward the mark for the prize of the high calling of God in Christ Jesus" (Phil. 3:13, 14).*

Prayer: Lord Jesus, thank you for this present moment. Help me to capture it and to live it to the fullest for you. I choose to forget those things in the past and to press on from this moment forward in your service. I choose to accept each succeeding moment as a gift from your hands.

Any sufferings in this present time are not worthy to be compared with the glory you will reveal in us.[1] Help me not to be preoccupied with either the past or the future but to live fully in the present moments of my life. The devil wants to distract me through guilt and fear, but I will not listen to him. Whether the world, or life, or death, or things present, or things to come, all are mine in you, Lord.[2] Nothing will be able to separate me from your love — not things past, present nor yet to come.[3] Praise your name, Jesus! I claim your promise and I appropriate it to my life in the NOW.

When your good chastening comes into my life, Lord, help me to remember that even though it does not seem pleasant in the present moment, nevertheless afterward it will yield the peaceable fruit of righteousness in my life. In such times, help me to lift up my hands and make straight paths for my feet.[4] I do so now, Lord, looking straight ahead and refusing to look back. I realize that I have put my hands to your plow, Lord; if I look back to the attractions of the old life, I cannot be fit for your kingdom.[5] In single-minded determination, therefore, I will keep pressing on.

You are the God of all grace, Father. Thank you for calling me unto your eternal glory by Christ Jesus. I know that when I suffer it will only last awhile, and in the process, you are perfecting, establishing and strengthening me. This is your present-moment work in my life, Lord. To your name be glory and dominion forever and ever.[6]

Help me to remember that the time is short[7] and must not be wasted. Let me redeem the time by walking circumspectly in each present moment because the days are evil.[8] Help me not to be unwise but to understand your will, Lord. Now is the accepted time. Now is the day of salvation.[9] I receive all you have for me in this present moment, Lord. Equip me to do your work effectively in these last days. In times past I walked according to the course of this world, but now I want to walk in your will and your righteousness. Thank you, Lord, for raising me up to sit together in heavenly places with you.[10]

You are the eternal I AM, Father. There is no past or future with you. Let me be a present-tense believer whose life is hidden with Christ in you.[11]

References: (1)Romans 8:18 (2)1 Corinthians 3:22 (3)Romans 8:38,39 (4)Hebrews 12:11-13 (5)Luke 9:62 (6)1 Peter 5:10,11 (7)1 Corinthians 7:29 (8)Ephesians 5:16 (9)2 Corinthians 6:2 (10)Ephesians 2:2-6 (11)Colossians 3:3
Other Scriptures: Galatians 4:2-5

FRUITFULNESS

14

Walking in Love

Key Thought: God is love.

Key Scripture: *"There is no fear in love; but perfect love casteth out fear: because fear hath torment. He that feareth is not made perfect in love. We love him, because he first loved us"* (*1 John 4:18-19*).

Prayer: Heavenly Father, you loved the world so much that you gave your only begotten Son, that whosoever would believe in Him should not perish, but have everlasting life.[1] Truly, there is no greater love. Thank you for sending Jesus to redeem this world, and for saving me.

Forgive me, Father, for my lack of love. Help me always to remember that I am able to love only because you first loved me.[2]

Loving you leads me into obedience, for you have pointed out that we will follow your commands if we truly love you.[3] Because you have saved me and made me a new creature, I can love others as you have loved me. And by this all men will know that I am your disciple.[4] I thank you that your perfect love has cast out all fear in my life,[2] and that I am learning how to love sincerely, without any hypocrisy.[5]

There is no limit to your love, Father. It is from everlasting to everlasting. Shed your love abroad in my heart[6] so that I may be able to comprehend with all saints the full extent of your love.[7]

Help me always to remember that love's immediate response is to give.[1] Because you are love it is possible for your love to flow through me to others. Help me to love, give and serve in your manner, Jesus Christ, my Lord.

Lord Jesus, you are dwelling in my heart by faith and you are rooting and grounding me in your love. Above all else, Lord, I desire to know your love which passes knowledge and to be filled with all your fullness.[7]

Love is the most excellent way.[8] It has supremacy over every other gift. I know, Lord, that you want me to walk in love, to love other people as you have loved me. I want to learn to love you, my Father, with all my heart, soul, mind and strength and to love my neighbor as myself.[9]

Lord, it is your love that knits my heart together with other believers.[10] Your love gives me a purpose for living and it always leads to joy. Now abides faith, hope and love; help me to realize that the greatest of these is love,[11] and to walk in love in all the relationships of my life.

Father, you commended your love toward me in that while I was yet a sinner, Jesus died for me.[12] Thank you, Lord, that you have shown me the key to love — that it is not merely an action or emotion, but a state of being. God, you *are* love.[13] As you live in me, may love become my nature, too.

References: (1)John 3:16 (2)1 John 4:17-21 (3)John 14:15
(4)John 13:34,35 (5)Romans 12:9 (6)Romans 5:5
(7)Ephesians 3:18-20 (8)1 Corinthians 12:31 (9)Mark 12:30,31
(10)Colossians 2:2 (11)1 Corinthians 13:13 (12)Romans 5:8
(13)1 John 4:7-11 **Other Scriptures:** John 15:13

15

Walking in Joy

Key Thought: God wants to fill you with joy.

Key Scripture: *"A merry heart maketh a cheerful countenance: but by sorrow of the heart the spirit is broken. The heart of him that hath understanding seeketh knowledge: but the mouth of fools feedeth on foolishness. All the days of the afflicted are evil; but he that is of a merry heart hath a continual feast" (Prov. 15:15).*

Prayer: Lord, it is your joy that gives me strength.[1] I'm so glad that you want me to have joy. You have not given me a spirit of fear, but you have introduced me to your kingdom where I find righteousness, peace and joy in the Holy Spirit.[2] You have given me joy unspeakable and full of glory as I receive the end of my faith — the salvation of my soul.[3] The joy of my salvation keeps me going, Thank you, Father.

I repent of all lack of joy that I have ever exhibited as your follower. I pray that others will see your joy in my life. I pray that you will continue to restore unto me the joy of your salvation.[4] Knowing you and your ways gives me great joy.

Your wonderful joy gives me all I need to keep on with what you have called me to do. I rejoice in you, Father, because of your goodness and love.[5] I joy in you through my Lord Jesus Christ, by whom I have received forgiveness of my sins, enabling me to be one with you. I desire to finish my course with joy,[6] looking unto you, Jesus, because you are the Author and Finisher of my faith.[7]

Therefore, with joy I draw water from the wells of salvation.[8] This is the day that you have made, Lord; I will rejoice and be glad in it.[9] I will praise your name, Lord, from this day forward, rejoicing always in your goodness to me. Praise the Lord!

A merry heart makes a cheerul countenance,[10] Lord, and I pray that others will see your joy in my face and life. I will greatly rejoice in you, Lord, and my soul will be joyful in you. You have clothed me with the garments of salvation and covered me with a robe of righteousness.[11]

Fill me with your wisdom and spiritual understanding, Lord, that I might walk worthy of you unto all pleasing, being fruitful in every good work, and increasing in the knowledge of God; strengthened with all might, according to your glorious power, unto all patience and longsuffering with joyfulness;[12] giving thanks unto you, Father, always and in all things.[13]

References: *(1)Nehemiah 8:10 (2)Romans 14:17 (3)1 Peter 1:8,9 (4)Psalms 51:12 (5)Psalms 5:11 (6)Acts 20:24 (7)Hebrews 12:2 (8)Isaiah 12:3 (9)Psalms 118:24 (10)Proverbs 15:13 (11)Isaiah 61:10 (12)Colossians 1:10-12 (13)Ephesians 5:20* **Other Scriptures:** *Psalms 16:11, Psalms 35:9, Psalms 48:2, Isaiah 49:13, John 15:11, Philippians 4:4-10*

16

Walking in Peace

Key Thought: The peace of God surpasses human understanding.

Key Scripture: *"And let the peace of God rule in your hearts, to the which ye are called in one body; and be ye thankful"* *(Col. 3:15).*

Prayer: Dear God, how I thank you for your peace which passes all understanding and keeps my heart and mind through Christ Jesus.[1] You keep me in perfect peace when my mind is stayed on you because I trust in you.[2] Your peace is so precious to me. Help me to trust you always.

Your peace in my heart is the umpire that tells me what's right and wrong. I ask you, Lord, to help me follow the guidance of your peace in my heart.[3]

Help me, insofar as it is possible, to live in peace with those outside the Body of Christ, as well as with my brothers and sisters in Christ.[4] Don't let me make excuses for strife and unforgiveness. Help me remember it takes two to quarrel and a soft answer turns away wrath.[5]

Keep my tongue from evil, and my lips from speaking guile. I seek and pursue peace with all my heart.[6] Lord Jesus, you are the Prince of Peace,[7] and I want to be your follower.

Help me to be a fruit-bearing Christian, Lord, one who shows forth the fruit of peace in all my relationships.[8] As I learn to live in the Spirit, help me to walk in peace[9] with you, God, with my fellow-man[10] and with myself. Peace is such a precious possession, and I want to guard it carefully. Teach me never to do anything that will disturb your precious peace.

I will trust in you forever because in you there is everlasting peace and strength.

When I follow your commandments, Lord, you promise to give peace like a river, and your righteousness as the waves of the sea.[11] Because I have been justified by faith, I will always have peace with you, Father, through my Lord Jesus Christ.[12]

Thank you, Jesus, for leaving your peace with me. You have imparted your peace to me through your Holy Spirit and I receive it now as I pray. Because you don't give as the world gives, I know the peace you've given to my heart will keep me from ever again being troubled or afraid.[13] Your peace makes me certain of all the truth of your Word. Thank you, Jesus.

References: (1)*Philippians 4:7* (2)*Isaiah 26:3,4* (3)*Colossians 3:15* (4)*Romans 12:18* (5)*Proverbs 15:1* (6)*Psalms 34:13,14* (7)*Isaiah 9:6* (8)*James 3:18* (9)*Galatians 5:25* (10)*Hebrews 12:14* (11)*Isaiah 48:18* (12)*Romans 5:1* (13)*John 14:27* **Other Scriptures:** *Psalms 29:11, Galatians 5:22*

17
Walking in Patience

Key Thought: God's timing is perfect.

Key Scripture: *"For ye have need of patience, that, after ye have done the will of God, ye might receive the promise"* *(Heb. 10:36).*

Prayer: Lord, I see my need for patience. Thank you for showing me that you are never in a hurry. Help me to learn to wait before you instead of being anxious.

I repent of all the times when I've wanted you to hurry up and of my unwillingness to wait for you. Forgive me for my impatience.

Help me to remember that the end of a matter is better than the beginning and that the patient in spirit is better than the proud in spirit. Teach me not to be hasty in my spirit with regard to anything.[1] I will learn to wait expectantly on you.

Let me be good ground, Lord, so that with a good and honest heart, I will hear your Word and keep it, and so bring forth fruit with patience.[2] You have commanded me to possess my soul through patience.[3] I will strive, therefore, to let patience have her perfect work in my life so that I might be found perfect and entire, wanting nothing.[4]

Laying aside every weight, and the sin which so easily besets me, I determine in my heart to run with patience the race you have set before me, always looking unto you, Jesus, the Author and Finisher of my faith.[5]

The promises of your Word cannot fail. How I thank you for those promises. Lord, it is my desire to do what you've called me to do. Help me to be content in well-doing, trusting you to bring the increase in every area of promise.[6]

I await your coming, Lord, with patience, as the husbandman waits for the precious fruit of the earth and has long patience for it. Teach me to be patient, Lord; to establish my heart, for your coming draws nigh.[7] Maranatha!

References: *(1)Ecclesiastes 7:8,9 (2)Luke 8:15 (3)Luke 21:19 (4)James 1:4 (5)Hebrews 12:1,2 (6)1 Timothy 6:6 (7)James 5:7,8,11* ***Other Scriptures:*** *Psalms 37:7, Psalms 40:1-3, Romans 5:3-5, Romans 15:5, Hebrews 6:12*

18
Walking in Gentleness

Key Thought: God is gentle. He is never rude. He wants us to become like Him. His Spirit produces the fruit of gentleness in my life.

Key Scripture: *"Thou hast also given me the shield of thy salvation; and thy right hand hath holden me up, and thy gentleness hath made me great" (Psalms 18:35).*

Prayer: Gentle and gracious Lord, sometimes it seems that the beautiful quality of gentleness is a forgotten trait in our present age. Like meekness and self-control, it is a fruit of your Holy Spirit,[1] and I thank you that you are developing the attribute of gentleness in my life.

Teach me to be truly gentle, Father. Forgive me for the times in my life when I have grown agitated in spirit, impatient, hasty and rude. I want to live my life in gentleness so that others will be drawn to you through my life.

Help me to be gentle with other people in my life in the same ways you have been gentle with me. Let gentleness sweeten all my dealings with others — my own family, the neighbors, the elderly, fellow-believers in the Body of Christ, and even those who oppose me.[2] Keep me from rudeness in each relationship or acquaintanceship, even with those who disappoint me.[3]

Help me to remember, Lord, that a meek and quiet spirit is of great value to you. Adorn the hidden man of my heart with your gentleness which is not corruptible.[4]

Help me not to confuse gentleness with weakness, but to view gentleness as a sign of strength. Thank you, Father, for giving us so many examples of the strength of gentleness in the Bible. The lives of David, Jacob, Stephen, John and Paul show forth your gentleness.[5] Lord Jesus, I thank you for your gentle spirit, for your kindness, meekness and strength.[6] Impart these same qualities to my spirit, Lord, and let me reflect your gentleness in all my ways.

References: (1)*Galatians 5:22* (2)*2 Timothy 2:24* (3)*Titus 3:2* (4)*1 Peter 3:4* (5)*2 Corinthians 6:1-10* (6)*2 Corinthians 10:1* **Other Scriptures:** *2 Samuel 22:36, 1 Thessalonians 2:7*

19

Walking in Goodness

Key Thought: All goodness comes from God.

Key Scripture: *"Surely goodness and mercy shall follow me all the days of my life: and I will dwell in the house of the Lord forever" (Ps. 23:6).*

Prayer: Heavenly Father, like the Psalmist, I taste and see that you are good![1] You are merciful and gracious, longsuffering, and abundant in goodness and truth.[2] I want my life to bear forth abundantly the fruit of your goodness.

O Lord God, you are the one true God, and your words are true. You have promised goodness to your servant.[3] You have assured me that your goodness and mercy will follow me all the days of my life.[4] Teach me the meaning of true goodness. Help me to see, Lord, that any goodness I possess stems directly from my relationship with you. In and of myself I possess no goodness,[5] but your life within me produces the fruit of goodness in my life. You alone are good, Lord.[6]

I rejoice in your goodness.[7] I choose to be glad and merry in heart for the goodness you have shown to me.[8] You have given me the faith to see your goodness in the land of the living.[9] How great is your goodness which you have laid up for them that fear you![10] Your goodness endures continually,[11] and you fill me with your goodness. You, Lord, satisfy the longing soul and fill the hungry soul with goodness.[12]

You promise goodness to all those who continue in your ways.[13] It is my earnest desire always to show forth your goodness. May your goodness lead me to knowledge, that I might be able to live godly and to admonish others in love.[14] As I endeavor to walk in the light as you are in the light,[15] I know you will fill me with goodness and righteousness and truth.[16]

I love you, Lord, for your exceeding goodness, and I thank you that your goodness is filling me.[17]

References: (1)Psalms 34:8 (2)Exodus 34:6 (3)2 Samuel 7:28
(4)Psalms 23:6 (5)Romans 7:18 (6)Luke 18:19 (7)2 Chronicles 6:41
(8)2 Chronicles 7:10 (9)Psalms 27:13 (10)Psalms 31:19
(11)Psalms 52:1 (12)Psalms 107:9 (13)Romans 11:22
(14)Romans 15:14 (15)1 John 1:7 (16)Ephesians 5:9
(17)Galatians 5:22 **Other Scriptures:** Psalms 144:2

20
Walking in Faithfulness

Key Thought: God is faithful. His Spirit produces the fruit of faithfulness in my life.

Key Scripture: *"His lord said unto him, Well done, good and faithful servant; thou hast been faithful over a few things, I will make thee ruler over many things: enter thou into the joy of thy lord"* (Matt. 25:23).

Prayer: Great is thy faithfulness, O God, my Father.[1] Your Word reveals the importance of faithfulness in my walk with you. Let this fruit of the Spirit grow in my life until I learn to be faithful in the little things. I realize, Lord, that until I can be faithful in small things, you cannot entrust me with the weightier matters of the Kingdom.[2]

You have shown me that faithfulness involves steadiness, consistency and stability,[3] and that these qualities come to me only as I learn to keep my priorities in order and my perspective straight. Lord, help me to see the importance of faithfulness in my life[4] — faithfulness to you, to other people, to my responsibilities and to myself — so that others will know they can depend on me, and so that the enemy has nothing in me.[5] Grant that I might never fail to see my need for faithfulness.

Forgive me for the times when I have failed to be faithful, Father. I realize now that faithfulness is the fruit of your Spirit in my life.[6] Be faithful through me, Lord. May others see your faithfulness exhibited in my life.

Teach me to be a good steward over all that you have entrusted to my care.[7] Keep me, Lord, from the error of seeing possessions, talents and family members as *mine*, because everything in the universe you created belongs to you.[8] Help me always to realize that my primary responsibility is to respond to *your ability* instead of striving through my own personal strength to accomplish your will. Use me to your greater glory, Lord, and make me a faithful manager over your property.

Thank you for your faithful mercies, O Lord. Your lovingkindness in my life is renewed each day. From this day forward, I determine to live my life in such a way, empowered by your Spirit, that others will see my faithfulness. I invite you to do whatever is necessary and to show me what I need to do to cause this fruit to develop fully in my life. Let me see that being faithful is being *full of faith.*

References: (1)Lamentations 3:23 (2)Luke 19:17 (3)2 Thessalonians 3:3 (4)Proverbs 28:20 (5)John 14:30 (6)Galatians 5:22 (7)Luke 12:37 (8)Psalms 24:1 Other Scriptures: Psalms 31:23, Proverbs 11:13, Proverbs 13:17, Proverbs 14:5, 1 Corinthians 1:9, Revelation 2:10

21

Walking in Meekness

Key Thought: Meekness is a spiritual temperament that says, "Yes," to God in joyful obedience. It is slow to give or take offense. It is teachable and rests upon the grace of humility.

Key Scripture: *"Take my yoke upon you, and learn of me; for I am meek and lowly of heart (humble): and you shall find rest unto your souls." (Matt. 11:29).*

Prayer: Lord, I gladly obey and take your yoke upon me that I may learn of you. Teach me meekness. Let this fruit of your Spirit grow in me daily.[1] I choose to walk worthy of the calling to which I have been called — with behavior which is a credit to the summons to your service.[2] To walk with complete lowliness of mind (humility) and meekness, with patience, bearing with others and making allowances for them in love.[3]

Lord, I now put on the new man, which is renewed in knowledge after the image of you, who created me.[4] I put on meekness, therefore, as the elect of God, holy and beloved.[5] Help me, Lord, to be slow to take offense at others and to patiently endure even when I am wrongfully persecuted.[6]

As your servant, help me not to strive, but to be apt to teach in meekness, instructing those who oppose themselves that they may be fully restored to you and your love.[7] Give me the grace to lay aside self-interest and to esteem others better and higher than myself. Help me to not look just on my own things but also on the things of others.[8]

Produce in me that quality of meekness that is pliable and teachable that I may receive with meekness your Word, which is able to save my soul.[9]

Lord, I commit to follow after righteousness, godliness, faith, love, patience and meekness. And to fight the good fight of faith and thereby lay hold on eternal life to which I am called.[10]

References: *(1)Galatians 5:23 (2)Ephesians 4:1 (3)Ephesians 4:2 (4)Colossians 3:10 (5)Colossians 3:12 (6)1 Peter 2:20 (7)2 Timothy 2:24,25 (8)Philippians 2:3,4 (9)James 1:21*

(10)1 Timothy 6:11,12 **Other Scriptures:** *Numbers 12:3, Matthew 5:5, 1 Corinthians 4:20,21, 2 Corinthians 10:1, 1 Timothy 6:11,12, Titus 3:2, 1 Peter 3:15*

22
Walking in Self-Control
(Temperance)

Key Thought: Self-control is a fruit of the Spirit.

Key Scripture: *"He that hath no rule over his own spirit is like a city that is broken down, and without walls"* *(Prov. 25:28).*

Prayer: Lord Jesus, I come to you with the realization that I need to exercise self-control in my life. Thank you for the gift of faith.[1] And thank you that to my faith, virtue is being added and, to my virtue, knowledge. Father, I ask you now to help me add temperance and self-control to my life. I know that if these things dwell within me, I will become fruitful in the knowledge of my Lord Jesus Christ. Without self-control, however, I quickly become spiritually blind, forgetting your grace, Lord Jesus.[2]

I do not want to be like a city that is broken down and without walls, O Lord. I repent of all the times when I've been intemperate and out-of-control.

Strengthen me by your Spirit, Lord, so that the fruit of self-control can develop in my life.[3] Thank you, Father. I accept this by faith, and I commit myself to cooperating with you as you bring self-control to fruition in my life.

You have set a race before me. I want to run the race of life with patience and temperance. Help me, Lord, to strive for the mastery in my life by being temperate in all things. It is the incorruptible crown of life that I seek.[4] Help me, therefore, to keep my body under subjection to my spirit, always looking unto Jesus who is the Author and Finisher of my faith.[5]

Lord, I hold fast the faithful word that you have given to me. Help me not to seek self-gratification, but to be just, holy and temperate.[6] I put on the breastplate of righteousness, and the helmet of salvation, realizing that these gifts from your hand will help me to be sober and vigilant.[7] Assist me to bring all my thoughts into the captivity of Christ.[8] May He truly control my life so that self-control will actually become the Master's control. Thank you for this precious fruit of your Holy Spirit.

References: *(1)Ephesians 2:8 (2)2 Peter 1:3-8 (3)Galatians 5:23 (4)1 Corinthians 9:24-27 (5)Hebrews 12:1,2 (6)Titus 1:7-9 (7)1 Thessalonians 5:6-8 (8)2 Corinthians 10:5* **Other Scriptures:** *Proverbs 16:32, 1 Peter 1:13, 1 Peter 4:7, 1 Peter 5:8,*

THE INNER LIFE

23

Walking in Blessedness

Key Thought: Blessed means happy and spiritually prosperous, experiencing God's favor.

Key Scripture: *"Even as David also describeth the blessedness of the man, unto whom God imputeth righteousness without works, saying, Blessed are they whose iniquities are forgiven, and whose sins are covered. Blessed is the man to whom the Lord will not impute sin"* *(Rom. 4:6-8).*

Prayer: Thank you, Lord, for wanting me to be happy. You love to bless your people and you have surely blessed me. Thank you for showing me the way to blessedness in this life. I am happy in your service, Lord.

The poor in spirit are happy because theirs is the kingdom of heaven. Make me poor in spirit, Lord, depending totally upon you.

Deliver me from the kingdom of self. I want to be clothed with your humility, Lord.

They who mourn are happy when you bring them comfort, because they realize you are their Source. The meek are happy because they will inherit the earth. Help me to become meek, Lord, and to seek you when I am in mourning.

You have shown us that all who hunger and thirst after righteousness are happy because they will be filled. Please increase my spiritual hunger and thirst for your righteousness. Even now you are filling me with all I need.

The merciful are happy because they have obtained mercy. Make me merciful, Lord, in all my relationships. Because the pure in heart shall see God, they are happy. I want to be pure in heart, Lord. Continue your workmanship in my life.

The peacemakers are happy because they shall be called the children of God. May I be known as a peacemaker, Lord, living in peace with everyone. All who are persecuted for your name's sake are happy too, Lord, because they know that their reward will be great in heaven. Help me to rejoice and be exceeding glad in the face of persecution, Lord.[1]

Help me never to faint in the day of adversity, but to be of good courage, knowing that you will strengthen my heart.[2] It is so good to know, Father, that my happiness is not based on the temporal circumstances of life.

I realize, Lord, that blessedness comes when one delights himself in your Word. I will meditate on your Word day and night. Keep me from walking in the counsel of the ungodly.[3] My hope and happiness are in you.

Because I've tasted and seen that you are good, Lord,[4] you have forgiven me of all my transgressions and I am truly blessed indeed. Thank you for the gift of blessedness.

References: (1)Matthew 5:1-12 (2)Proverbs 24:10 (3)Psalms 1:1 (4)Psalms 34:8 **Other Scriptures:** Psalms 2:12, Psalms 32:1, Psalms 84:5, Proverbs 8:34, Matthew 24:46, John 13:17, John 20:29, Acts 20:35, Acts 26:2, Romans 14:22, James 1:12, 1 Peter 3:14, 1 Peter 4:14, Revelation 22:14

24
Walking in Confidence

Key Thought: Confidence comes from knowing God hears and intervenes.

Key Scripture: *"For thus saith the Lord God, the Holy One of Israel; In returning and rest shall ye be saved; in quietness and in confidence shall be your strength" (Isa. 30:15)*

Prayer: In quiet confidence I come before your throne of grace, Lord, knowing that there I will find grace and mercy in my time of need.[1] Teach me to be still and to know that you are God — the one, true God who hears and answers prayer.[2] This is the key to my confidence in you, Lord — that your Word promises if I ask anything according to your will, you hear me, and if you hear me, I know I have what I have asked.[3] To ask in your will I must know your will and be willing to obey it. Then my heart will not condemn me, and I can have confidence toward you that whatever I ask, I will receive, because I keep your commandments and do those things which are pleasing to you.[4] Now, I can confidently enter your rest, that special place of certain confidence that comes from believing in you, obeying your voice, and knowing you hear my prayers.

Thank you for always being there and for being the same yesterday, today, and forever.[5] You have promised never to leave me nor forsake me and have assured me that you will be with me until the end of the age.[6] I know, Lord, that with you there is no variableness, neither shadow of turning. Thank you, Lord Jesus. These facts of my faith give me confidence.[7]

I am certain in my confidence that you have saved me, Lord; your Word tells me that if I believe on the name of

Jesus Christ and receive Him as my Lord, I have eternal life.[8] I have done this and I know I am saved and I am a child of God. I know you are at work in my life because I see your hand at work. I have confidence in you because of all you have done for me and all I see you doing. I will walk confidently before you in the land of the living.[9]

Keep my heart from condemnation, Lord; there is no condemnation to those who are in you, who walk not after the flesh but after the Spirit.[10]

Lord, I want all my confidence to be in you.[11] I never want to place confidence in the flesh.[12] The answer to any problem I face in life lies in worshiping you in the spirit and rejoicing in Christ Jesus always.[13] I confidently rejoice in you, my Lord.

References: *(1)Hebrews 4:16 (2)Psalms 46:10 (3)1 John 5:10-15 (4)1 John 3:21,22 (5)Hebrews 13:8 (6)Hebrews 13:5 (7)Ephesians 3:12 (8)John 1:12, John 3:16 (9)Psalms 116:9 (10)Romans 8:1 (11)Proverbs 3:26 (12)Philippians 3:3,4 (13)Philippians 4:4* **Other Scriptures:** *Proverbs 14:26, 2 Thessalonians 3:4, Acts 16:31, Romans 10:9,10, Hebrews 3:14, Hebrews 3:6, James 1:17*

25

Glorifying the Lord

Key Thought: The chief end of man is to glorify the Lord and enjoy Him forever.

Key Scripture: *"Let your light so shine before men, that they may see your good works, and glorify your Father which is in heaven"* (Matt. 5:16).

Prayer: Lord Jesus, it is your light that shines within me and brings glory to the Father. Let me be a light shining in the darkness of our sinful world. May other people glorify you, Father, when they see the life of Jesus in me.[1]

Father, glorify your name through my life.[2] May others see your power and glory reflected in me. I know that I have been bought with a price; therefore, I desire to glorify you in my body and in my spirit which are yours.[3]

When others behold good works in my life may they glorify you in the day of visitation.[4] I recognize my responsibility to honor and glorify you for all the things I have heard and seen.[5] Glory to God in the highest, and on earth peace, goodwill toward men.[6]

Teach me your way, O Lord. I will walk in your truth. Unite my heart to fear your name. I will praise you, O Lord, for you are my God. I will glorify your name forevermore.[7] Glory to God in the highest. Glory to your name.

Whoso offers praise glorifies you, O Lord.[8] I praise you and adore you with all my heart. May I be found worthy of your high calling, Lord, and fulfill all the good pleasure of your goodness. May I serve you in faith and in power so that your name will be glorified in my life, according to the grace you have imparted to me.[9]

Help your people to be likeminded so that we all may with one mind and one voice glorify you in all the earth.[10] Hallelujah!

References: *(1)Matthew 5:16 (2)John 12:28 (3)1 Corinthians 6:20 (4)1 Peter 2:12 (5)Luke 2:20 (6)Luke 2:14 (7)Psalms 86:11,12 (8)Psalms 50:23 (9)2 Thessalonians 1:11,12 (10)Romans 15:6* **Other Scriptures:** *Acts 4:21*

26

Walking in Hope

Key Thought: Hope is a light that shines through the darkness.

Key Scripture: *"To whom God would make known what is the riches of the glory of this mystery among the Gentiles; which is Christ in you, the hope of glory: Whom we preach, warning every man, and teaching every man in wisdom; that we may present every man perfect in Christ Jesus"* *(Col. 1:27-28).*

Prayer: Lord Jesus Christ, you are my hope.[1] My hope is built solidly on you, my Rock. Blessed be God the Father who has begotten me, according to His abundant mercy, unto a lively hope by the resurrection of Jesus from the dead. You have given me hope, Lord, of an inheritance incorruptible, and undefiled, and that never fades away. It is reserved in heaven for me![2]

You are building your house, Lord, and I thank you that you have included me in your plans. Help me always to hold fast the confidence and the rejoicing of hope firm unto the end.[3] You have given me the full assurance of this plan.[4] The hope you have imparted unto me is the anchor of my soul, Lord. It makes my life sure and steadfast. Rejoicing in hope, Lord, I can be patient in tribulation and continue instant in prayer.[5]

My faith and hope are completely in you, Lord.[6] I sanctify you, setting you apart, Lord, in my heart, and I am ready always to give an answer to everyone who asks for a reason of the hope that is within me. Let me always answer in meekness and fear of you.[7]

I know, Lord, that, when you shall appear, I will be like you, for I will see you as you are. Because I have this hope, my heart is purified.[8] Thank you, Jesus. Thank you for the gift of hope.

References: (1)1 Timothy 1:1 (2)1 Peter 1:3 (3)Hebrews 3:6 (4)Hebrews 6:11 (5)Romans 12:12 (6)1 Peter 1:21 (7)1 Peter 3:15 (8)1 John 3:2,3 Other Scriptures: Titus 2:13, Titus 3:7, Hebrews 6:18, Hebrews 7:19

27

Walking in Humility

Key Thought: God enters lives through humble hearts.

Key Scripture: *"Let nothing be done through strife or vainglory; but in lowliness of mind let each esteem other better than themselves" (Phil. 2:3).*

Prayer: Lord, you have commanded your people to humble themselves and turn from their wicked ways. When we do this, and when we seek your face, your Word declares you will hear from heaven and heal our land.[1] Lord, help me to walk in humility so that my prayers will be answered. In an attitude of humility, my heart sees its need for you in all things.

Your Word tells me that you will turn your face toward those who are of a poor and contrite spirit, toward those who tremble at your Word.[2] In the light of your Word I see that, apart from you, I am poor and wretched. I also see that in Christ you have made me a new creation, raised me to newness of life[3] and made me a partaker of your divine nature.[4] Therefore, I can walk in true humility.

The sacrifices that are acceptable to you, Father, are a broken spirit. A broken and a contrite heart, O God, you will not despise.[5] I desire to be a broken vessel that you can use, so I humbly beseech you to so work in my life that I will have a broken and a contrite heart.

By humility and the fear of the Lord riches, honor and life are imparted. The fear of the Lord is the instruction of wisdom; and before honor is humility.[6] Instruct me, Lord, that I will know how to seek wisdom and honor by the route of humility and in no other way. Help me to see how true humility and the fear of the Lord work together with the power of your Word.

In humility, Lord, I recommit my life to serving you with many tears of repentance and compassion for others. Your Word tells me to be clothed with humility because you resist the proud and give grace to the humble. In view of this, I willingly humble myself under your mighty hand, knowing that you will exalt me, Father, in due time.[7] And keep me ever mindful, Lord, that being exalted by you and being exalted in the eyes of the world are not necessarily synonymous.

Voluntarily, I submit myself to you, Lord, and with determination, I resist the devil. I know these two acts will cause the enemy to flee from me. As I draw near to you, Father, you are drawing near to me.[8] The key to all these blessings is humility in the sight of the Lord, and the end result is that you always lift me up.[9] Thank you, Lord.

References: *(1)2 Chronicles 7:14 (2)Isaiah 66:1,2 (3)Romans 6:4 (4)2 Peter 1:4 (5)Psalms 51:17 (6)Proverbs 15:33 (7)1 Peter 5:5,6 (8)James 4:6-10 (9)Job 22:29* *Other Scriptures:* *Proverbs 16:19, Proverbs 22:4, Matthew 18:4, Philippians 2:1-10*

28
Walking in Integrity

Key Thought: Personal integrity is priceless.

Key Scripture: *"The integrity of the upright shall guide them: but the perverseness of transgressors shall destroy them"* *(Prov. 11:3).*

Prayer: Heavenly Father, strengthen my character by enabling me to conquer every temptation. As you help me to be true to what I know is right, I will be able to walk in integrity of heart.[1] Let my integrity guide me in every situation; may it rule in the face of every temptation.

All the temptations I face are common to people. You are strong when I am tempted, Lord, and you give me strength. You provide me with a way to escape that enables me to bear up in the face of testings and trials.[2] You always make your grace abound in my life,[3] and this leads me to walk in integrity. I want to have a consistent walk before you and others, Lord.

Fill me with integrity of heart, Lord. Help me always to be like Jesus who refused to abandon His integrity in the midst of difficult circumstances.[4]

Keep my soul, Lord, and deliver me. Let me not be ashamed to have put my trust in you. Let integrity and uprightness preserve me, for I wait on you.[5]

With your help, Father, I will walk in integrity. Redeem me, and be merciful unto me.[6] You feed me according to the integrity of your heart and you guide me by the skillfulness of your hands.[7] May your integrity and your skill emanate from my life.

Help me to see that the issues of life spring from the heart, and as a man thinks in his heart, so is he.[8] Give me the grace to keep my heart with all diligence, Lord,[9] and the willingness always to act in accord with what my heart knows is right.

Your counsel in my heart is like deep water. May I be a person of understanding who lets your counsel flow from my life. May I never proclaim my own goodness. Rather, I want to be a faithful person[10] who is just and filled with the integrity that comes from you.

References: *(1)Genesis 20:6 (2)1 Corinthians 10:13 (3)2 Corinthians 9:8 (4)Job 27:5 (5)Psalms 25:21 (6)Psalms 26:11 (7)Psalms 78:72 (8)Proverbs 23:7 (9)Proverbs 4:23 (10)Proverbs 20:5,6* **Other Scriptures:** *Genesis 20:5, Proverbs 11:3, Daniel 1:8, Daniel 3:17,18, Daniel 6:7,9,10,16,22*

29

Knowing God

Key Thought: The difference between knowing God and knowing about Him is vast.

Key Scripture: *"That I may know him, and the power of his resurrection, and the fellowship of his sufferings, being made conformable unto his death" (Phil. 3:10).*

Prayer: Dear Lord, like Paul, I want my life theme to be to know you in all your fullness and power. As I bow in your presence, I am still, and this is when I know that you are God.[1] You will be exalted in the earth. I want to know you in all your fullness and power, Lord.

You want everyone to know you, Lord. What a wonder and a privilege it is to know, that as your servant, I can actually come to know you and have fellowship with you. No longer do you call me your servant, Lord, but you have designated me to be your friend. Thank you, Jesus. You have chosen me as your friend.[2] You have even promised to betroth me in faithfulness,[3] and in this way I can know you in an intimate, personal way.

You have promised that the people who know you will be strong and do exploits through you.[4] Praise you, God! I receive your strength to do exploits in your name. So many get weary of the journey, Lord, but I want to be one who follows on to know you. Your going forth is prepared as the morning; and you will come to me as the rain, as the latter and former rain unto the earth.[5]

Help me to teach your ways to others so that others will know you, Lord, from the least to the greatest.[6] Lord Jesus, you are the propitiation for our sins. How do I know that I know you, Lord? Your Word tells me if I keep your commandments, I will learn to know you intimately.[7]

Obedience demonstrates my love for you. Help me remember the importance of conducting my life in such a way that others will realize I know you.

As I open my life to you, Lord, I ask you to fill me with the knowledge of your will in all wisdom and spiritual understanding; that I might walk worthy of you unto all pleasing, being fruitful in every good work, and increasing in the knowledge of you.[8] Father, thank you that I can know you, the Master and Creator of the universe, personally and intimately.

References: *(1)Psalms 46:10 (2)John 15:15 (3)Hosea 2:20 (4)Daniel 11:32 (5)Hosea 6:3 (6)Hebrews 8:11 (7)1 John 2:3 (8)Colossians 1:9,10* **Other Scriptures:** *Ezekiel 38:16, Hosea 8:2, Mark 1:24, Philippians 3:10*

30
Walking in Praise

Key Thought: Praising God leads me into His presence.

Key Scripture: *"Enter into his gates with thanksgiving, and into his courts with praise: be thankful unto him, and bless his name. For the Lord is good; his mercy is everlasting; and his truth endureth to all generations" (Ps. 100:4-5).*

Prayer: Lord God, I praise you and adore you. You alone are worthy of praise for you are the Creator of all things.[1] In you all things hold together.[2] Thank you, Lord; I bless your name; I rejoice in your mercy and truth.

I will sing unto you; I will sing praise to you, the Lord God of Israel.[3] In trust and obedience I praise your name. I will praise you, Lord, according to your righteousness; I will sing praise to your name, O Lord most high.[4]

I will praise your name forever. When I offer praise to you, Lord, you are glorified.[5] This brings us both great joy and blessing. Let my mouth be filled with your praise and honor all day long.[6]

I will sing of your mercies forever. With my mouth will I make known your faithfulness to all generations.[7] It is such a good thing to give thanks unto you, O Lord, and to sing praises unto your name. I want to show forth your lovingkindness in the morning and your faithfulness every night.[8]

Because of who you are, and all you've done for me, I am able to offer the sacrifice of praise to you continually. It pleases me, Lord, to be able to give you the fruit of my lips, even praise to your name.[9]

You have blessed me with gifts of communication, Lord. How I thank you and praise you for the ability to praise. In everything I do may you be glorified. Lord Jesus, praise and dominion belong to you for ever and ever.[10]

Joining with the angel chorus, I glorify you, Lord. Alleluia! The Lord God omnipotent reigns! You are the King of kings and Lord of lords![11]

References: (1)*John 1:3* (2)*Colossians 1:17* (3)*Judges 5:3* (4)*Psalms 7:17* (5)*Psalms 50:23* (6)*Psalms 71:8* (7)*Psalms 89:1* (8)*Psalms 92:1,2* (9)*Hebrews 13:15* (10)*1 Peter 4:11* (11)*Revelation 19:6,16* **Other Scriptures:** *Nehemiah 12:24, Psalms 44:8, Psalms 95:1,2 Psalms 100*

31

Learning to Pray

Key Thought: Prayer is a sustaining power in our daily lives.

Key Scripture: *"Praying always with all prayer and supplication in the Spirit, and watching thereunto with all perseverance and supplication for all saints" (Eph. 6:18).*

Prayer: Praise waits for you, O God, in Zion, and unto you shall all my vows be performed. You are the One who hears my prayers, and unto you shall all flesh come.[1] I come to you, Father, with the request, "Teach me to pray."

Lord Jesus, when your disciples asked you to help them to learn to pray, you gave the perfect example of the life of prayer.[2] You prayed without ceasing[3] and you brought all your requests before the Father.[4]

I thank you for the direct-line access I now have to you, Father, through my Lord Jesus Christ. He is the one mediator between you and me,[5] and because He obeyed you even unto death, I now have access to you through prayer. I thank you, Father, for the fellowship I can have with you and with your Son, Jesus Christ.[6]

I know you hear my prayers, Lord. Because I know you hear me, I have confidence that I will receive the petitions I have asked of you.[7] You want me to humble myself and pray and seek your face and turn from my wicked ways.[8] This I want to do, Lord, and I thank you that you hear me from heaven, as I repent before you in humility to receive your cleansing, refreshing and fellowship.

I give myself to a life of prayer,[9] because I know that so many things are accomplished through prayer. I am thankful that the prayer of the upright is your delight,[10] O Lord. Without any anxiety, therefore, I make my requests known unto you in everything by prayer and supplication with thanksgiving.[4]

Your Word is filled with so many precious prayer promises. I thank you, Lord, that as I meditate on those promises and pray your Word and will, your Word will not return unto you void. It will accomplish your purposes.[11]

It is through prayer that I get to know you, Lord, and all my heart's desire is to know you better, for to know you in the right way is eternal life and in your presence is fullness of joy and pleasures forevermore.[12]

References: (1)*Psalms 65:1,2* (2)*Matthew 6:9-15*
(3)*1 Thessalonians 5:17* (4)*Philippians 4:6* (5)*1 Timothy 2:5*
(6)*1 John 1:3,9* (7)*1 John 5:14,15* (8)*2 Chronicles 7:12-14*
(9)*Psalms 109:4* (10)*Proverbs 15:8* (11)*Isaiah 55:11*
(12)*Psalms 16:11* *Other Scriptures:* *2 Kings 20:5, Psalms 4:1*

32

Rejoicing in the Lord

Key Thought: The joy of the Lord is my strength.

Key Scripture: *"That the trial of your faith, being much more precious than gold that perisheth, though it be tried with fire, might be found unto praise and honour and glory at the appearing of Jesus Christ: Whom having not seen, ye love; in whom, though now ye see him not, yet believing, ye rejoice with joy unspeakable and full of glory"* (1 Pet. 1:7-8).

Prayer: Lord Jesus Christ, I rejoice in you with exceeding great joy because of all you've done for me and because of who you are.[1] In everything I give you thanks, for this is the will of God for me. Help me, Lord, to rejoice evermore and to pray without ceasing.[2]

Alleluia! The Lord God omnipotent reigns! I am glad, therefore, and rejoice, and give honor to you![3] You alone are worthy to receive honor and glory, O Lord.[4] I choose to magnify and exalt you. I enter your gates with thanksgiving and proceed into your courts with praise.[5]

Thank you, Jesus, for being my Lord and my God, for working your purposes out, in and through my life. I make a joyful noise unto you and serve you with gladness. I come before your presence with singing. I am thankful that I know you are Lord; it is you who made me, and I am your child. Praise your mighty name![5]

I am thankful unto you, O Lord, and I bless your name because you are good. Your mercy is everlasting, and your truth endures to all generations.[6] Hallelujah!

Lord, I rejoice inasmuch as I am a partaker of your sufferings. I know that when your glory is revealed I will be glad with exceeding great joy.[7] This knowledge enables me to count it all joy when I fall into diverse temptations, because I know that the trying of my faith will develop patience within me.[8] Praise God!

You are so great, dear God, and you are greatly to be praised. I will bless you with all that is within me.[9] Bless your holy name![10]

References: (1)Philippians 3:1 (2)1 Thessalonians 5:16-18 (3)Revelation 19:7 (4)Revelation 4:11 (5)Psalms 100 (6)Psalms 117:2 (7)1 Peter 4:13 (8)James 1:2 (9)Psalms 103:1 (10)Psalms 34:1-3 *Other Scriptures:* Nehemiah 8:10, Nehemiah 12:43, Isaiah 35:2, Luke 10:17-20, 1 Peter 1:8

33

Entering God's Rest

Key Thought: Trusting in God brings rest to the soul.

Key Scripture: *"There remaineth therefore a rest to the people of God. For he that is entered into his rest, he also* *hath ceased from his own works, as God did from his. Let us labour therefore to enter into that rest, lest any man fall after the same example of unbelief" (Heb.4:9-11).*

Prayer: Lord Jesus, thank you for your rest. Your Word shows me that it is impossible to remain in your rest if I grow hard in heart, walk in unbelief or disobey. Keep me from all hardness of heart, unbelief and disobedience, Lord.[1] Forgive me where I have failed you in any of these areas.

You have given your promise that I may enter into your rest. Help me to cease from my own works, Lord, and to let you take over every aspect of my life. Keep me from trying so hard in my own strength that I fail to trust in you. Help me to understand that the real labor of the spiritual life is to enter into your rest.[2]

Thank you for your invitation, Lord Jesus, to come to you when I am weary and heavy laden, knowing that you will give me rest. I do so now, and I take your yoke upon me to learn of you. You are meek and lowly in heart and in you I will find rest unto my soul. Your yoke is easy and your burden is light.[3]

Like King David, I would set you always before me. With you at my right hand, I will not be moved. Therefore, my heart is glad and my glory rejoices. My flesh rests in your hope, Father.[4] You will show me the path of life. In your presence there is fulness of joy. At your right hand there are pleasures forevermore.[5]

I rest in you, Lord. I will wait patiently for you. I trust and delight in you, and I commit my way unto you.[6] You give the weary rest and you bring refreshing to the heart that trusts in you.[7] Thank you for being my safe place of refuge[8] and rest.

My heart is still, at rest in you. I know that you are my God.[9]

References: *(1)Hebrews 3:6-19 (2)Hebrews 4:1-11*
(3)Matthew 11:28-30 (4)Psalms 16:8,9 (5)Psalms 16:11
(6)Psalms 37:4-7 (7)Isaiah 28:12 (8)Psalms 46:11 (9)Psalms 46:10
Other Scriptures: *Psalms 95:11*

34
Seeking God

Key Thought: Seeking leads to spiritual discoveries.

Key Scripture: *"Sing unto him, sing psalms unto him, talk ye of all his wondrous works. Glory ye in his holy name: let the heart of them rejoice that seek the Lord. Seek the Lord and his strength, seek his face continually"* (1 Chron. 16:9-11).

Prayer: Lord, I seek you with all my heart. I will always seek you, knowing that I will surely find you when I seek your face continually.[1] When I draw near to you, I know you will draw near to me.[2]

You are my God, and early I will seek you. Every morning I will seek you. My soul thirsts for you. I desire to see your power and your glory. Your lovingkindness is better than life. Therefore, my lips shall praise you and I will bless you.[3]

I sing of you, Lord, and I talk of all your wondrous works. I glory in your holy name as my heart rejoices while I seek you and your strength.[4] When I ask of you, I will receive. When I seek, I will find. When I knock, it shall be opened unto me.[5] Thank you, Lord.

You have revealed so many things to me by your Spirit, O Lord. Mighty things, which I could not know apart from seeking you, have been revealed to me. It is so wonderful to know you and to learn your ways.[6]

What joy there is in realizing that I am risen with you, Lord Jesus. Because this is true, I commit my life to seeking those things which are above, where you sit on the right hand of the Father. I set my affections on things above, not on the things of the earth.[7] I seek those things that have eternal value.

You are a rewarder of all who diligently seek you.[8] Thank you, Lord. As I sow in your righteousness, I reap in mercy. Help me to break up the fallow ground in my life, for I know it is time to seek you with all my heart. Soon you will come, Lord, and you will rain righteousness upon your people.[9] Thank you for coming to me when I seek you.

References: *(1)Deuteronomy 4:29 (2)James 4:8 (3)Psalms 63:1-4 (4)Psalms 105:2-4 (5)Matthew 7:7 (6)Jeremiah 33:3 (7)Colossians 3:1,2 (8)Hebrews 11:6 (9)Hosea 10:12* *Other Scriptures:* *2 Chronicles 15:2, Psalms 22:26, Jeremiah 29:13, Matthew 6:33*

35
Walking in Trust

Key Thought: Trust and obey; there's no other way.

Key Scripture: *"Trust in the Lord with all thine heart; and lean not unto thine own understanding. In all thy ways acknowledge him, and he shall direct thy paths"* *(Prov. 3:5-6).*

Prayer: Heavenly Father, because my heart is fixed, trusting in you, I will not be afraid of any evil tidings.[1] I want to grow in my ability to trust you, because I know that true joy and blessing come from trusting in you with all my heart.

You promise that anyone who trusts in you will be like a tree planted by the waters, that spreads out its roots by the river.[2] You also promise to direct the paths of a person who trusts in you with all his heart.[3] Still another blessing that comes from trusting you is that mercy will encompass me.[4] Thank you, Father, for your great faithfulness that leads me to trust in you. These wonderful truths about walking in trust cause me to be glad in you, Lord, and to rejoice because you are watching over me.

Trusting in you, Father, I will continue in supplications and prayers night and day.[5] Grant that I would never place my trust in uncertain riches or any other thing except the living God, who richly gives us all things to enjoy.[6]

As I learn to trust you, Lord, I pray that you will help me to build other relationships in my life based on trust. All trust comes through Christ, and, as I turn toward you, I realize that I am not sufficient of myself in anything, but my sufficiency is of God who has made me an able minister of the New Testament.[7]

I place all my trust in you, O Lord. Thank you for all you are doing in my life to foster my trust in you and my trustworthiness before you.

References: (1)Psalms 112:7 (2)Jeremiah 17:7,8 (3)Proverbs 3:6 (4)Psalms 32:10,11 (5)1 Timothy 5:5 (6)1 Timothy 6:17,18 (7)2 Corinthians 3:4-6 Other Scriptures: 2 Samuel 22:3, Psalms 7:1, Psalms 37:3, Nahum 1:7, 1 Timothy 4:10

36
Walking in the Will of God

Key Thought: God's way is perfect.

Key Scripture: *"I delight to do thy will, O my God: yea, thy law is within my heart" (Ps. 40:8).*

Prayer: Thank you for revealing your will to me, Father, through the Scriptures and the life of your Son. You have poured out your Spirit upon me and you have promised to make your words known unto me.[1] I desire to know your will, and I delight to do your will.

Help me to have the same attitude that exists in you, Christ Jesus, my Lord, to be able to say to the Father, "Your will be done."[2] Thank you for accepting me into your family; you have stated that whoever does the will of your Father in heaven is your brother, sister and mother.[3]

Father, forgive me for the times when I have left the security of being in your will. In those times, Lord, I've learned that there is no better place to be than in the center of your perfect will. I repent of all the self-will in my life. Help me to remember that of my own self I can do nothing. I know that my judgment will be just only if I seek your will, Father, rather than my own will.[4]

Thank you, Jesus, for revealing God's will to me. I know that it is your will that all should come to a saving knowledge of your truth[5] and that in you are hid all the treasures of wisdom and knowledge.[6] If I will be diligent to seek you, the Father will reward me with those precious treasures and I will be better able to win souls to you.[7] It is the Father's will that you, Lord Jesus, would lose nothing that He has given to you. It is His will that all who come to believe in you will have everlasting life, and He will raise all believers at the last day.[8] Praise your name, Lord! Teach me how to leave things in your hands, Lord, especially when there is nothing else I can do about a given situation. In knowing your will, Lord, I can learn to approve the things that are more excellent, being instructed out of your Word.[9]

Lord, you have abounded toward me in all wisdom and prudence; you have made the mystery of your will known unto me, according to your good pleasure which you have purposed in yourself. Thank you for giving me the inheritance of being predestinated according to your purpose and for working all things after the counsel of your will. I know that it is your will, Father, that I would be found to the praise of your glory because I have trusted in you.[10]

References: (1)Proverbs 1:23 (2)Luke 22:42 (3)Matthew 12:50 (4)John 5:30 (5)2 Peter 3:9 (6)Colossians 2:3 (7)Hebrews 11:6 (8)John 6:37,38 (9)Romans 2:18 (10)Ephesians 1:4-14
Other Scriptures: John 3:16, John 17:12, Acts 21:14

37
Walking in the Word

Key Thought: The Bible is a living book.

Key Scripture: *"For the word of God is quick, and powerful, and sharper than any two-edged sword, piercing even to the dividing asunder of soul and spirit, and of the joints and marrow, and is a discerner of the thoughts and intents of the heart" (Heb. 4:12).*

Prayer: Thank you for your Word, Father. It is a light unto my path and a lamp unto my feet.[1] Teach me to study your Word so that I can show myself approved unto you, a workman who never needs to be ashamed because I have learned to divide your Word rightly.[2] I will search the Scriptures daily to discover your truth and direction.

Your Word will not depart out of my mouth, Lord. I will meditate upon it day and night so I will learn to walk in your Word daily. When this becomes a reality in my life, Lord, you will make my way prosperous and fill my life with success.[3] Thank you for this promise which so encourages me.

You have performed your Word over and over again, Lord.[4] You have confimed it to my heart so many times in my life. May your Word always be with me as I learn to hide it in my heart so I will not sin against you.[5] Help me to use your Word as the sword of your Spirit, the weapon through which I will always be able to stay the hand of the enemy.[6]

Lord, your way is perfect and your Word is tried; you are a mighty buckler to all who trust in you.[7] It is your precious Word that brings faith to my heart and gives me the ability to trust you. Speak to me through the pages of the Scriptures and strengthen my faith.

Your wonderful Word makes me wise unto salvation. May it always have free course in my life. Your Word is like the rain and the snow that come forth from heaven and do not return, but they water and sustain the earth. The water of your Word cleanses me, sustains me, and it will not return unto you void. It will accomplish all that you please in my life.[8]

Your Word gives me life[9] because it is the Word of Life. I am reminded, Lord, by your Word, that death and life are in the power of my tongue[10] and that when I speak your Word, I speak forth life into my own heart and the hearts of others. As I hold forth your Word, help me to rejoice in the day of Christ, knowing that my labor is not in vain in you, O Lord.[11] I want to become a doer of your Word, Father, and not just a hearer only, thereby deceiving myself.[12] By keeping your Word, your love is made perfect in me. Give me the grace, Lord, to be both a doer and a keeper of your Word.[13]

References: *(1)Psalms 119:105 (2)2 Timothy 2:15 (3)Joshua 1:8 (4)1 Kings 8:20 (5)Psalms 119:9-11 (6)Ephesians 6:17*

(7)*Psalms 18:30* (8)*Isaiah 55:10,11* (9)*Psalms 119:50*
(10)*Proverbs 18:21* (11)*Philippians 2:16* (12)*James 1:22*
(13)*1 John 2:5* **Other Scriptures:** *2 Kings 3:12,*
2 Chronicles 10:15, Proverbs 30:5, Romans 10:17, 2 Timothy 3:15

38
Worshiping the Lord

Key Thought: Awareness of who God is leads to worship.

Key Scripture: *"God is a spirit: and they that worship him must worship him in spirit and in truth" (John 4:24).*

Prayer: You are the One who lives forever, and you are worthy, O Lord, to receive glory and honor and power. You created all things, and for your pleasure they are and were created.[1] This knowledge leads me to worship you. Thank you for creating me for your pleasure. I want to bless you and please you.

God, my Father, teach me how to be a worshiper in spirit and in truth. I want to be a true worshiper because I know that this is what you seek in my life.[2] My spirit yearns to be in your presence. In your presence there is fulness of joy.[3]

If I am to worship in spirit and truth, Lord, I realize that I must worship in honesty and candor about where I am spiritually[4] and also that I must worship through your Word, for your Word is truth.[5]

And teach me to be a listener, Lord;[6] it seems so much easier to be a talker[7] or a doer. One of the lessons in your story of Mary and Martha, Lord, is that sitting at your feet and listening is worship and it is the one needful thing in my life.[8] May I never forget to take time each day to sit at your footstool and worship you. I bow my heart before you. I adore you and honor you. Father, I magnify your name.

When I realize all you have done for me, I am compelled to worship you. As I worship you, I rejoice in every good thing that you have given me.[9] I rejoice in you, Lord. Being in your presence through worship is life's most wonderful blessing.

As you grant repentance to my heart, I turn to you in worship and adoration. I give unto you, Lord, the glory that is due your name. I come before you and worship you in the beauty of holiness.[10] You are my Father. I love you, and as I draw near to you, you fill my heart with glory. Heavenly Father, I appreciate you.

I turn my eyes upon you, O Lord, and the things of earth grow strangely dim in the light of your glory and grace. Worshiping you lifts me above my problems and gives me a new perspective on your ability to perfect all things concerning me. Hallelujah!

I worship you, O Lord, and bow down. I kneel before you, my Maker, for you are my God, and I am one sheep of your pasture.[11]

God, I thank you that you have created me to worship you. Teach me to be a worshiper in spirit and truth.[2] I will spend as much time as possible each day basking in your presence and seeking your face. Thank you for the practical benefits of worship.

References: (1)*Revelation 4:10,11* (2)*John 4:23* (3)*Psalms 16:11* (4)*John 3:21* (5)*John 17:17* (6)*Psalms 46:10* (7)*Matthew 6:7* (8)*Luke 10:42* (9)*Deuteronomy 26:9-11* (10)*1 Chronicles 16:29* (11)*Psalms 95:6,7* *Other Scriptures:* *1 Samuel 15:25, Philippians 3:3, Revelation 5:14*

PRAYERS THAT PREVAIL

PART II

Prayers for Personal Concerns

A. Emotional Health

B. Spiritual Growth

C. Health and Happiness

EMOTIONAL HEALTH

39

Freedom From Addictions

Key Thought: You do not have to be in bondage to anything.

Key Scripture: *"Stand fast therefore in the liberty wherewith Christ hath made us free, and be not entangled again with the yoke of bondage" (Gal. 5:1)*

Prayer: Lord Jesus, you came to preach the gospel to the poor, heal the brokenhearted, preach deliverance to the captives and recovering of sight to the blind. You have also promised to set at liberty those who are bruised.[1] I acknowledge that my addiction to _____ _____ has made me a captive and has bruised me in many ways. More than that, Lord, you know that this addiction is really not the root of my problem — it is only a symptom of the real root which is my hurt, rejection, bitterness, resentment, and lack of esteem and love for myself. I know this is not your will for me to be captive to any addiction and that you desire to be Lord in every area of my life. I ask you to come in power and deliver me now as I pray.

Lord, if there is any sin in my life that has opened the door to this addiction, show it to me. If there is any unforgiveness, bitterness or judgment of others, any evil speaking, hatred of others or myself, any wrath, sinful anger, jealousy or any other sins, reveal them to me now, and I will confess and repent of them so that you may heal me. As you show me my sin(s), I say, "Yes, that is sin," and I confess it/them as sin and turn from it/them in deep heartfelt repentance. I ask your forgiveness for these sins. Thank you, Lord, that you are now cleansing me from these sins and all unrighteousness by your blood.[2]

If there are any unhealed wounds or hurts in my life that are doorways for this addiction, show them to me so I may acknowledge them as true. I am willing to face the truth you bring, Lord, because you said the truth will make me free.[3] As you show me these wounds and hurts now, Lord, I say, "Yes, Lord, bring your healing love to my heart and heal each wound and hurt."[4] I receive your healing touch now, Lord.

Lord, I repent specifically of the sin of this addiction of _____. I renounce it now, Lord. I realize that repentance prepares the way for you to work in my life. Because you are my Lord, the power of sin and addiction is broken in my life. At the name of Jesus every knee must bow, including the knee of addiction.[5]

Because I was buried with Christ in His death, I can now walk in newness of life.[6] In Christ I am dead to sin and alive to God. Therefore, I will not let the sin of addiction reign in my mortal body nor will I obey the lusts of it.[7]

Lord, you resist the proud and give grace to the humble.[8] I humble myself before you now.[9] I come boldly to your throne of grace. I ask for grace to help me in this time of need.[10] Father, I ask you to intervene in my life. Strengthen me by your Spirit in my inner man.[11] Now as I pray your Word, I receive your healing touch[12] that delivers me from the bondage of this addiction. I renounce it now, Lord. Because of your mercy it will not have any power over me any longer.[13] You are my Lord and I submit my life totally to you.

Father, I thank you that the dark power of addiction over me is broken. You have translated me out of the power of darkness into the kingdom of your Son, my Lord, Jesus Christ.[14]

Lord, I thank you that you never leave me.[15] I thank you for your guiding presence and your love. Sustain me, Lord, whenever I am tempted to fall back into addictive habit patterns. For you will always show me the way of escape.[16] Thank you for pouring out your Spirit upon me and for giving me total victory.

Thank you, Father, for setting me free. I have entered the glorious liberty of the sons of God.[17] I will not be addicted to _____ any longer. Praise you, Jesus!

References: *(1)Luke 4:18 (2)1 John 1:9 (3)John 8:32*
(4)Psalms 147:3 (5)Philippians 2:10 (6)Romans 6:1-4
(7)Romans 6:11,12 (8)James 4:6 (9)1 Peter 5:6 (10)Hebrews
4:15,16
(11)Ephesians 3:16 (12)Psalms 107:20 (13)Psalms 51:1
(14)Colossians 1:13 (15)Hebrews 13:5 (16)1 Corinthians 10:13
(17)Romans 8:21 **Other Scriptures:** *Psalms 119:45, Isaiah 61:1,*
Matthew 8:17, Matthew 22:37-39, John 3:16, John 14:15,
Romans 8:5-7, Romans 14:11, 2 Corinthians 10:4-6,
Galatians 5:13, Galatians 5:17-21, Philippians 2:13, James 1:25,
Revelation 3:19

40

Freedom From Anger

Key Thought: Unresolved anger leads to depression.
Key Scripture: *"Mortify therefore your members which are upon the earth; fornication, uncleanness, inordinate*

affection, evil concupiscence, and covetousness, which is idolatry...But now ye also put off all these; anger, wrath, malice, blasphemy, filthy communication out of your mouth...And put on the new man, which is renewed in knowledge after the image of him that created him" (Col. 3:5, 8-10).

Prayer: Lord, you are a God who is ready to pardon, gracious and merciful, slow to anger, and of great kindness.[1] You are renewing my life so that I am becoming more like you.[2] Thank you, Father. I renounce the power anger has held over my life, and I repent of the sins into which it has led me.

Lord, I pray for _____ who have received the brunt of my anger and fury. Heal their hurts, Lord, and let them know that your love covers a multitude of sins.

It is your will for me to cease from anger and forsake wrath because those who do evil will be cut off, but those who wait on you will inherit the earth.[3] My earnest prayer is that you will help me cease from anger and forsake all wrath in my life. Show me how to avoid sinful anger. May I never let the sun go down on my wrath.[4] Teach me how to deal constructively with the anger I experience, through forgiveness, openness and honesty.

Help me to remember your words of wisdom: that a soft answer will turn away wrath but grievous words will stir it up.[5] Set a watch before my lips, O Lord,[6] and help me to bridle my tongue.[7] The tongue of the wise uses your knowledge in the right way, but the mouth of fools pours out foolishness.[5]

Lord, you have shown me that he who is slow to anger is better than the mighty, and he who rules his spirit is better than he who takes a city.[8] It is my desire to be in control of my spirit so that I will be slow to anger, as you are.

May I never grieve your Holy Spirit by whom I have been sealed unto the day of redemption. Lord, let all bitterness and wrath and anger, and clamor, and evil speaking be removed from my life. Replace those sinful responses with the fruit of your Spirit, that I might be kind to others, tenderhearted, forgiving, even as you have forgiven me for Christ's sake.[9]

References: (1)Nehemiah 9:17 (2)Romans 8:29 (3)Psalms 37:8,9 (4)Ephesians 4:26 (5)Proverbs 15:1-4 (6)Psalms 141:3 (7)James 3:2 (8)Proverbs 16:32 (9)Ephesians 4:30-32

41
Freedom From Bitterness

Key Thought: Become better, not bitter.

Key Scripture: *"Looking diligently lest any man fail of the grace of God; lest any root of bitterness springing up trouble you, and thereby many be defiled" (Heb.12:15).*

Prayer: Heavenly Father, I know there is no place for bitterness in a believer's life. Your grace makes it possible for me to be free from all bitterness and resentment. Thank you, Lord.

You offer light to everyone who is in misery, and life unto the bitter in soul.[1] It is bitterness that leads to envy and strife, and when a believer engages in such behavior he is lying against the truth.[2] The people who crucified you, Lord Jesus, were full of bitterness and rage.[3] It blinded them from the truth and they continued in bitterness until their deaths. There is such defilement in bitterness and it has the power to destroy people's lives. Lord, I never want to deny your truth through bitterness or any other sin.

In your Word you show how the heart knows its own bitterness,[4] resulting in loneliness and joylessness. May I never permit bitterness to enter my soul.[5] Whenever I am tempted to become bitter, please be there to lead me to repentance, Lord, so that the thoughts of my heart may be forgiven and I will avoid the gall of bitterness and the bonds of iniquity.[6] Those who choose to live in bitterness have mouths full of cursing and their feet are swift to shed blood. They have not known the way of peace, and they have no fear of God.[7]

Uproot any bitter seeds that the devil desires to cultivate in my life. I will guard against all forces of bitterness around me with the sweetness of your Spirit, Lord.

Bitterness grieves the Holy Spirit by whom I have been sealed unto the day of redemption.[8] Therefore, I commit my life to putting away all bitterness, and wrath, and anger, and malice, and clamor, and all evil speaking. I choose rather to work toward kindness, being tender-hearted and forgiving, even as you have forgiven me for Christ's sake.[9] Thank you, Father.

References: (1)Job 3:20 (2)James 3:14 (3)Zechariah 12:10 (4)Proverbs 14:10 (5)Isaiah 38:15 (6)Acts 8:23 (7)Romans 3:14-18 (8)Ephesians 1:13,14 (9)Ephesians 4:31 Other Scriptures: Isaiah 38:17

42

Freedom From Complaining

Key Thought: There is no place for complaining in the Lord's service.

Key Scripture: *"Do all things without murmurings and disputings: That ye may be blameless and harmless, the sons of God, without rebuke, in the midst of a crooked and perverse nation, among whom ye shine as lights in the world; Holding forth the word of life" (Phil. 2:14-16).*

Prayer: Dear Lord, what an honor it is to be your servant, holding forth your Word of life to a crooked and perverse generation. Keep me from all grumbling, complaining and murmuring as I do your service. I resolve to delight in doing your will and to rejoice in you always.

Whenever I complain, my spirit becomes troubled and agitated.[1] I know this is not your will for me, because you want me to walk in peace. Peace comes to me whenever I submit to your will and trust in you.

Lord, when your people complained in the days of their wandering in the wilderness, it displeased you.[2] Help me always to remember that you see me and hear me wherever I am.[3] I never want to displease you in my thoughts, words, or actions.

I realize, Lord, that murmurers and complainers are walking after their own lusts.[4] This is so far removed from your ways and your words. Whenever I hear someone complaining, help me to keep from entering into their ways, but to remember your ways and to follow them. Help me to encourage those who are negative by always exhibiting a positive faith in you.

Instead of complaining, I will remember your benefits to me.[5] I will review the many ways in which you have dealt bountifully with me.[6] Thank you for your grace and your love.

Keep me positive, Lord. Instead of getting caught up in the negative forces of life, I want to think about the good things of you. You are good, Lord, and greatly to be praised.[7] Nothing is impossible with you.[8] Any sufferings in this present time are not worthy to be compared with the glory you will reveal.[9]

Because you have set your love upon me I will serve you with joy. When times get hard, I will continue to call upon you. I know you will answer me and you will be with me in times of trouble. You will deliver me from grumbling and complaining. With long life you will satisfy me and show your salvation unto me.[10] Thank you, Lord.

References: (1)*Psalms 77:3* (2)*Numbers 11:1* (3)*Exodus 16:8,9* (4)*Jude 16* (5)*Psalms 103:2* (6)*Psalms 116:7* (7)*Psalms 48:1* (8)*Matthew 19:26* (9)*Romans 8:18* (10)*Psalms 91:15,16*
Other Scriptures: *Numbers 16:41, Numbers 17:5,10, Psalms 77:3, Psalms 142:2, John 6:43, 1 Corinthians 10:10, Philippians 4:4*

43
Freedom From Condemnation

Key Thought: There is no condemnation to those who believe on Christ Jesus.

Key Scripture: *"For God sent not his Son into the world to condemn the world; but that the world through him might be saved. He that believeth on him is not condemned: but he that believeth not is condemned already, because he hath not believed in the name of the only begotten Son of God (John 3:16-18).*

Prayer: Thank you, Lord Jesus, that I do not have to live in condemnation any longer. There is no condemnation to me because I am in you. I no longer walk after the flesh, but after the Spirit. For the law of the Spirit of life in Christ Jesus has made me free from the law of sin and death.[1]

I come against the enemy of my soul who would have me feel cast down and dejected. Through the power of your

Spirit, Lord, I reject the lies and accusations of the father of lies[2] and the accuser of the brethren.[3] It is his deception that causes me to feel condemned. Keep me from falling into the condemnation of the devil, Lord. His desire is to trip me up and ensnare me. I choose to believe in you instead of him, and I know that by resisting him in faith, he will flee from me.[4] Thank you, Lord, for setting me free from all feelings of condemnation. I know I'm free, indeed. Your truth has set me free.[5]

When I lived under the law of sin and death, you came to me and said, "Neither do I condemn you: go, and sin no more."[6] You commended your love to me, in that while I was yet a sinner, you died for me.[7] Such amazing love has no parallel.

Thank you for your promise, Lord, that assures me that, if I hear your Word and believe on you, I have everlasting life. I will not come into condemnation; I have passed from death to life.[8] Praise God!

The ministry of your Spirit in my life is so glorious. It so far exceeds the experience of condemnation that it is not worthy to be compared to it. Your ministry of righteousness in my life exceeds in glory.[9] I thank you, God, for setting me free from condemnation.

References: *(1)Romans 8:1,2 (2)John 8:44 (3)Revelation 12:10 (4)James 4:7 (5)John 8:32 (6)John 8:11 (7)Romans 5:8 (8)John 5:24 (9)2 Corinthians 3:9* **Other Scriptures:** *Luke 6:37, Romans 2:1, 1 Timothy 3:6*

44

Freedom From Depression

Key Thought: Let the Light of life shine in the midst of your darkness.

Key Scripture: *"Why art thou cast down, O my soul? and why art thou disquieted within me? hope in God: for I shall yet praise him, who is the health of my countenance, and my God" (Ps. 43:5).*

Prayer: Lord, you are my Shepherd. Yea, though I walk through the valley of the shadow of death, I will fear no evil: for you are with me. Your rod and your staff comfort me.[1]

I confess my depression to you, and in so doing I forsake it, putting it behind me forever. You have lifted me from the miry clay and set my feet upon the solid confidence of your Word.[2] I will not give in to depression any longer. Instead, I choose to hope and trust in you.

I will trust in you with all my heart, and lean not to my own understanding. In all my ways I will acknowledge you and you will direct my paths.[3]

You are the God of my strength. There is no reason for me to mourn because of the oppression of the enemy. I will go to you, unto God, my exceeding joy. I will praise you, Lord.[4]

As the deer pants after the water brooks, so my soul pants after you, my God. My soul thirsts for you, for the living God. My tears have been my meat day and night. My soul is cast down within me, but I will yet remember you. Deep calleth unto deep at the noise of your waterspouts and the stormy waves overwhelm me, yet I know you will command your lovingkindness to reach me. Your song will return to me. I will pray to the God of my life.[5]

I will say to you, my Rock, that you are my help, my strength, my hope, the health of my countenance, my Lord. You are freeing me from all sadness and depression. Praise your holy name.

You, Lord, are a shield for me. You are my glory and the lifter of my head. As I cry unto you, you hear me out of your holy hill.[6] Lord, you will sustain me. Hallelujah!

Lord, I know you have heard my prayer and seen my tears. You have promised to set me free and to heal me of my depression.[7] You have delivered my soul from death, my eyes from tears and my feet from falling. I will walk before you in the land of the living.[8]

I cried unto you, O Lord. You have brought up my soul from the grave. You have kept me alive, that I should not go down to the pit. You have turned my mourning into dancing to the end that my glory may sing praise to you, and not be silent. O Lord my God, I will give thanks to you forever.

References: *(1)Psalms 23 (2)Psalms 40:2 (3)Proverbs 3:5,6 (4)Psalms 43:2-4 (5)Psalms 42 (6)Psalms 3:3,4 (7)2 Kings 20:5 (8)Psalms 116:8,9* **Other Scriptures:** *Isaiah 38:5, Isaiah 61:3, Lamentations 5:15-19, Jeremiah 31:13*

45

Freedom From Fear

Key Thought: Faith dissipates fear.

Key Scripture: *"Behold, God is my salvation; I will trust, and not be afraid: for the Lord Jehovah is my strength and my song; he also is become my salvation. Therefore with joy shall ye draw water out of the wells of salvation. And in that day shall ye say, Praise the Lord"* (Isa. 12:2-4).

Prayer: Father, I thank you that you are my light and my salvation. Of what, then, shall I be afraid? You are the strength of my life; of whom shall I be afraid?[1] I will not be afraid of sudden fear, for you, Lord, are my confidence and you will keep my foot from being taken.[2]

You have given me peace and you have told me, "Don't let your heart be troubled and don't let your heart be afraid."[3] Thank you for your gift of peace through your Son, Jesus.

I have not received the spirit of bondage again to fear; but I have received the Spirit of adoption that causes me to cry, "Abba, Father." Thank you for making me your child.[4] Father, you are my helper; I will not fear what man can do to me.[5]

There is no fear in your love, Father. Your perfect love casts out all fear.[6] Thank you for delivering me from the torments of fear. Fill me with your love now as I receive it by faith in your promise.

As I seek you, Lord, I know that you hear me, and you are delivering me from all fear.[7] I will not fear because you are with me, and you have promised to bless me.[8] I refuse all fear as I stand still and see your salvation.[9] You, Lord, will fight for me and give me peace. I will not fear nor be discouraged, for you are with me[10] and you have not given me a spirit of fear, but of power and of love and of a sound mind.[11]

I renounce all the fears of my life, Lord. Through the power of your Spirit, I will no longer fear _____. These fears no longer have any power in my life. Hallelujah! You have set me free from my fears!

Lord, you are my refuge and my strength, a very present help in trouble. Therefore, I will not fear, though the earth be removed and though the mountains be carried into the midst of the sea.[12] I will fear no evil; for you are with me and your rod and staff bring me comfort.[13]

It is so good to know that I have no need to fear because you are my God. I will be glad and rejoice, for you, Father, will do good things in my life.[14] You have told me not to fear because it is your pleasure to give me your kingdom,[15] which is righteousness, peace and joy in your Holy Spirit.[16] Alleluia!

References: (1)Psalms 27:1 (2)Proverbs 3:25,26 (3)John 14:27 (4)Romans 8:15,16 (5)Hebrews 13:6 (6)1 John 4:18 (7)Psalms 34:4 (8)Genesis 26:24 (9)Exodus 14:13 (10)Deuteronomy 1:21 (11)2 Timothy 1:7 (12)Psalms 46:1,2 (13)Psalms 23:4 (14)Joel 2:21 (15)Luke 12:32 (16)Romans 14:17 Other Scriptures: Isaiah 12:2, Isaiah 44:8, Luke 8:50

46
Walking in Forgiveness

Key Thought: Because God has forgiven us, we need to forgive others.

Key Scripture: *"Let all bitterness, and wrath, and anger, and clamour, and evil speaking, be put away from you, with all malice: And be ye kind one to another, tenderhearted, forgiving one another, even as God for Christ's sake hath forgiven you" (Eph. 4:31-32).*

Prayer: Lord, you have taught us how to pray. You prayed, "Forgive us our debts, as we forgive our debtors."[1] It is my desire to forgive others in the same way you have forgiven me. Help me to walk in that kind of forgiveness, Lord.[2] Forgive me wherein I have failed to walk in forgiveness.

By an act of faith, Lord, I now forgive _____ _____ who has/have created problems in my life. I pray for him/her/them now, and I ask you to set him/her/them free from any bondage caused by my lack of forgiveness.

Your Word declares that if I will forgive the trespasses of others, you will forgive my trespasses. I know I need to forgive my brother seventy times seven, and more.[3] Teach me to forgive my brothers and sisters from my heart.[4]

Lord, when I do not forgive someone who has hurt me, I harbor hatred in my heart. This is not your way. I will always beware lest any root of bitterness springing up within me would defile me and others,[5] for I do not want to defile that which you have cleansed and purified through your precious blood and your Word.

When I pray, Lord, help me to remember when anyone might have something against me. At such times, help me to respond by going to my brother or sister and asking him/her to forgive me.[6]

Only because of your grace and forgiveness, O Lord, am I able to put on, as the elect of God, holy and beloved, bowels of mercies, kindness, humbleness of mind, meekness, and longsuffering. You enable me to forbear with others, and to forgive others when they wrong me.[7] This is my commitment to you, Father, and to the other people in my life.

Lord, even when I may suffer wrongfully, help me to be forgiving. For this is thankworthy, if a man for conscience toward God, should be wrongly accused and remain forgiving. I know there is no glory in my taking buffeting for my faults patiently; but when I do well, and suffer for it, and take it patiently, this is acceptable with you.[8]

Thank you for calling me to suffer in behalf of Christ. All who live godly in you will suffer persecution.[9] But, Lord, you suffered for us, leaving us an example, that we should follow in your steps.[8] Teach me your way in all things, especially in forgiveness.

References: (1)Matthew 6:12 (2)Mark 11:24-26 (3)Matthew 18:21,22 (4)Matthew 18:35 (5)Hebrews 12:15 (6)Matthew 5:23,24 (7)Colossians 3:12-16 (8)1 Peter 2:19-24 (9)2 Timothy 3:12
Other Scriptures: John 15:3, 1 John 1:7,9

47

Walking in Freedom

Key Thought: I'm free from the guilt of the past and I'm free from the fear of the future.

Key Scripture: *"Stand fast therefore in the liberty wherewith Christ hath made us free, and be not entangled again with the yoke of bondage" (Gal. 5:1).*

Prayer: Your death on the cross, Lord Jesus, has enabled me to enter the glorious liberty of the sons of God.[1] You have set me free from the bondages of sin and death. Hallelujah! What a Savior you are! I treasure the freedom you have given to me.[2]

Thank you, Father, for anointing Jesus to preach good tidings to the meek; to bind up the brokenhearted, *to proclaim liberty to the captives,* and the opening of prison to them that are bound.[3] Because of you I am no longer a captive to sin, and no longer a prisoner of darkness. Satan had me bound, but you have set me free!

You have set at liberty all who have been bruised, Lord.[4] Help me always to be certain that I will never allow the wonderful freedom you have given to me to become a stumblingblock to those who are weak.[5] Keep me walking in your freedom, Lord; keep me from ever being entangled again with any yoke of bondage.[2]

Thank you for sending your Spirit to be with me. Where the Spirit of the Lord is, there is liberty.[6] His presence in my life sets me free. Lead me into new dimensions of your freedom, Lord.

Thank you for calling me to liberty. Help me never to use the freedom you have given to me for an occasion to the flesh, but by love to serve others.[7]

As I look into your perfect law of liberty, Lord, I desire to continue in it as a doer of your Word, not a forgetful hearer. In doing so, I know that you will bless what I do.[8]

Thank you for showing me that it is your will for me to put to silence the ignorance of foolish men by well-doing. Not using my liberty as a cloak of maliciousness, but freely serving you, I will honor all men and love the brotherhood.[9]

Freely I have received from your hands, Lord, freely let me give.[10] May others find your freedom as I walk in freedom before them.

References: (1)*Romans 8:21* (2)*Galatians 5:1* (3)*Isaiah 61:1,2* (4)*Luke 4:18* (5)*1 Corinthians 8:7-13* (6)*2 Corinthians 3:17,18* (7)*Galatians 5:13,14* (8)*James 1:25-27* (9)*1 Peter 2:15* (10)*Matthew 10:8*

48

Freedom From Gossip

Key Thought: A little gossip goes far.

Key Scripture: *"Even so the tongue is a little member, and boasteth great things. Behold, how great a matter a little fire kindleth! And the tongue is a fire, a world of iniquity: so is the tongue among our members, that it defileth the whole body, and setteth on fire the course of nature; and it is set on fire of hell"* (James 3:5-6).

Prayer: Lord, thank you for the gift of speech. Help me to use it responsibly. Put a watch before my lips, Lord,[1] that I might always honor you with my words.

Lord, your Word says that a wholesome tongue is a tree of life, but perverseness therein is a breach in the spirit. Lord, so work in my life and my spirit that my tongue will be wholesome.[2] I commit myself to avoiding all gossip,[3] slander,[4] backbiting, whispering,[5] and malicious talk.[6] Help me to control my tongue, Lord, for in it is the power of death and life.[7]

You have described the ungodly as someone who has a burning fire in his lips. Keep me from ever sowing strife, Lord, for I know that a whisperer separates close friends.[8] May no form of corrupt communication ever leave my lips.[9] I repent of every misuse of speech in which I've engaged during my life. I renounce all gossip I've shared, and I put gossiping behind me forever.

When I encounter someone who is gossiping, help me to use the meeting as an opportunity to remind others of God's ways and to remind myself of my need to avoid all such conversations. Teach me, Lord, and I will hold my tongue.[10] Let my words always bring edification; may they be seasoned with your grace.[11]

Whenever I am tempted to gossip about another person, help me to use the opportunity as a call to prayer. Instead of gossiping about another person, lead me to pray for him/her so that you will intervene in his/her area of need. And, Lord, never let me stumble into using group prayer times or public prayer as a channel of gossip.

May I always walk uprightly,[12] speaking the truth in love and thereby grow up into Christ.[13] My tongue shall speak of your Word, Lord, and my lips will utter praise.[14] You have promised the love of life and good days to all who refrain their tongues from evil. Lord, I want to be certain that my lips never speak guile or evil things or gossip.[15]

Thank you for the wisdom and revelation you have given to me in the knowledge of you, Lord.[16] Because of those gifts, I am able to show out of a good conversation your ways and words in my life.[17] Out of the abundance of my heart, my words come;[18] may that abundance be treasures from your Word that I have sealed in my heart.

References: (1)*Psalms 141:3* (2)*Proverbs 15:4* (3)*1 Timothy 5:14*
(4)*1 Timothy 3:11* (5)*1 Corinthians 12:20* (6)*Romans 1:29*
(7)*Proverbs 18:21* (8)*Proverbs 16:27,28* (9)*Ephesians 4:29*
(10)*Job 6:24* (11)*Colossians 4:6* (12)*Psalms 15:2* (13)*Ephesians 4:15*
(14)*Psalms 119:172* (15)*1 Peter 3:10* (16)*Ephesians 1:17*
(17)*James 3:13* (18)*Matthew 12:34* *Other Scriptures:* *Psalms 34:13*

49

Freedom From Guilt

Key Thought: God has forgiven you.

Key Scripture: *"If we confess our sins, he is faithful and just to forgive us our sins, and to cleanse us from all unrighteousness"* (1 John 1:9).

Prayer: Thank you, Father, for forgiving me of my sins. As you have promised, when I sin I have an advocate with you, who is Jesus Christ the righteous: He is the propitiation for my sins, and not for my sins only, but also for the sins of the entire world.[1] You have granted repentance to my heart, I have turned from my sins, and I determine always to follow you. Because of your sacrifice, Lord Jesus, I am now one with the Father.

By taking heed to your Word, O Lord, I can keep myself from sin. With my whole heart I will seek you; don't let me wander from your commandments. I have hidden your Word in my heart that I might not sin against you.[2]

Guilt no longer has any dominion in my life. You, Lord Jesus, have set me free from guilt. Your sacrifice for my sins cleansed me from all sin, and now it is as if I had never sinned. Thank you for imputing your righteousness to me. Lord Jesus, you who knew no sin became sin for me that I might be made the righteousness of God in you.[3] Hallelujah!

Unto you, O Lord, I lift up my soul, for you are good, and always ready to forgive. You are plenteous in mercy unto all who call upon you.[4]

Thank you for forgiving me of my iniquities and for remembering them no more. Lord, you have removed my sins from me as far as the east is from the west;[5] you have buried them in the depths of the deepest sea. Help me to be like you in not remembering my sins anymore, either.[6] I am forgiven. I am restored. May I never dig up what you have buried, Father.

You have not dealt with me after my sins, nor rewarded me according to my iniquities. For as the heaven is high above the earth, so great is your mercy toward all who fear you.[7] Your mercy, O Lord, is from everlasting to everlasting upon those who fear you.[8] Praise your holy name.

From this day forward, Father, I covenant with you to put away from my life all bitterness, and wrath, and anger, and clamour, and evil speaking, with all malice. I will always endeavor to be kind to others, tenderhearted, forgiving others, even as you for Christ's sake have forgiven me.[9]

References: *(1)1 John 2:1,2 (2)Psalms 119:9-11 (3)2 Corinthians 5:21 (4)Psalms 86:4-6 (5)Psalms 103:12 (6)Hebrews 8:12 (7)Psalms 103:8-11 (8)Psalms 103:17 (9)Ephesians 4:30-32*
Other Scriptures: *Leviticus 4:35, Psalms 32:1, Luke 6:37, Luke 23:14,24*

50

Freedom From Jealousy
(Envy)

Key Thought: God's love overcomes jealousy.

Key Scripture: *"A sound heart is the life of the flesh; but envy, the rottenness of the bones"* (Prov. 14:30).

Prayer: Lord, I know it is not your will for me to fall prey to envy, jealousy or covetousness.[1] Instead, you want me to learn to love others. Help me to remember that love is patient and kind; love never envies.[2] Forgive me for being jealous and envious of other people, their possessions and their positions. I repent of my jealousy, envy and covetousness.[3]

As I take heed to your Word, I learn how to beware of covetousness and jealousy. A man's life does not consist in the abundance of things he possesses,[4] but in living for you.

Father, I thank you for the gift of godliness. It is so true that godliness with contentment is great gain. I brought nothing into this world and it is certain that I will carry nothing out.[5] You supply all my needs according to your riches in glory by Christ Jesus.[6]

Thank you for showing me that the love of money is the root of all evil. Grant that I will never fall into its snare. Rather, Lord, I desire to follow after righteousness, godliness, patience, faith, love and meekness with all those who live for you.[7]

Teach me never to envy other people. I want to learn how to be content in whatsoever state I find myself; to know both how to be abased and how to abound.[8] I trust you, Father, to lead me in the way that you know is best for me.

You have taught me, Father, that envy and jealousy come from pride. Through your strength I will be able to conquer the pride of life and the lusts of the flesh.[9] It is only the kindness and love of your Son that enables me to find freedom from jealousy; it is not through works of righteousness that I have done. Your mercy, Lord, has saved me and set me free.[10] Praise your name.

I determine in my heart, by faith in you, to walk in freedom from envy, Lord. Keep me from falling into its ungodly snare.

References: (1)Titus 3:3 (2)1 Corinthians 13:4 (3)Exodus 20:17 (4)Luke 12:15 (5)1 Timothy 6:6-8 (6)Philippians 4:19 (7)1 Timothy 6:10-12 (8)Philippians 4:11,12 (9)1 John 2:16 (10)Titus 3:5

51

Freedom From Loneliness

Key Thought: There is One who is always there.

Key Scripture: *"Let your conversation be without covetousness; and be content with such things as ye have: for he hath said, I will never leave thee, nor forsake thee"* (Heb. 13:5).

Prayer: Lord, thank you for your promise that you will be with me forever.[1] You did not leave me comfortless, but have sent your Spirit to be with me. Lord Jesus, you prayed to the Father, and He gave me your Spirit to be with me always. He is the Spirit of truth whom the world cannot receive, because the world does not see Him or know Him.[2] Thank you for sending Him and permitting me to know Him. He dwells within me, praise God!

Lord Jesus, when you were left alone in the Garden, you turned to your Father.[3] When you felt so alone on the cross, you turned to your Father.[4] Teach me to pray when I feel alone. Teach me to remember that you are always there.

You are my High Priest, and you do understand. Because of these realities, I hold fast to my profession in spite of loneliness, realizing, Lord, that you are touched with the feeling of my infirmities. You were tempted to feel alone just as I have been, but you turned to the throne of grace. Help me to remember that I will find mercy, comfort and grace there also, to help in my time of need.[5]

Everyone forsook you and fled, Lord Jesus, but you did not despair.[6] I know you understand how I feel. It is so wonderful to be able to walk with you. Let all loneliness that the enemy brings be gone from me, Lord. Tear down any thought strongholds of loneliness as I pray now.

My fellowship is with you, Father, and with your Son, Jesus Christ. Help me always to remember this truth so that my joy may be full.[7] May I never forsake the assembling I need with other believers as a member of your household.[8] Help me always to reach out to other people because I know the way to have friends is to be friendly,[9] and help me remember that, when I have fellowship with you, I will have a natural fellowship with other believers.[7] The Body of Christ is my spiritual family.

How I praise you and thank you, Father, that you are lifting loneliness from me. Its clouds have been dissipated by the sunshine of your love. I will never allow loneliness to darken my path again.

References: (1)Hebrews 13:5 (2)John 14:16-18 (3)Luke 22:41,42 (4)Luke 23:34,46 (5)Hebrews 4:14-16 (6)Mark 14:50 (7)1 John 1:3,4 (8)Hebrews 10:25 (9)Proverbs 18:24
Other Scriptures: Mark 15:34

52

Freedom From Lust

Key Thought: Lust leads to sin.

Key Scripture: *"But every man is tempted, when he is drawn away of his own lust, and enticed. Then when lust hath conceived, it bringeth forth sin: and sin, when it is finished, bringeth forth death" (James 1:14-15).*

Prayer: Heavenly Father, the lust of the eye and the lust of the flesh create great problems in life. When I am tempted in these areas, help me to remember that my temptation is common to man. This truth does not give me an excuse for yielding, however, because you have declared that you will always be faithful to me and you will not permit me to be tempted above my ability to resist. You will always, with the temptation, make a way for me to escape, so that I will be able to bear it.[1] Thank you, Lord.

Thank you for giving us so many examples of what happens when a person lusts.[2] Help me to learn from the teachings of your Word that warn us to flee lust. Above all, Father, keep me aware of my need for you in all things, to take heed, lest when I think I'm able to stand on my own, I fall.[1]

As I flee from lust, Lord, I ask you to empower me to follow righteousness, faith, charity (love) and peace with all who call on you out of a pure heart.[3] I will abstain from all fleshly lusts which war against my soul[4] and I will hide your Word in my heart that I might not sin against you.[5]

Help me to love not the world, neither the things that are in the world. Let your love fill me instead, Father, as I remember that all that is in the world — the lust of the flesh, the lust of the eyes, and the pride of life — are not of you, but of the world. Thank you for showing me that the world and its lusts will pass away, but he who does your will shall never pass away.[6]

As I seek *first* your kingdom and your righteousness, I learn to put all lust behind me.[7] Forgive me, Lord, for the idolatry of lust in my life; for failing to put you first.

Thank you for your grace that teaches me to deny all ungodliness and wordly lusts so that I might live soberly, righteously and godly in this present world. I choose, dear Lord, to look for that blessed hope and the glorious appearing of our Savior.[8]

I will walk in your Spirit, Lord, and by so doing, I will no longer fulfill the lusts of my flesh. Through the power of your Spirit, I mortify the deeds of my body and I crucify the old nature of my life with all its lusts and problems.[9] I will walk in spiritual freedom and victory, Lord, because you have overcome the the world.[10]

References: (1)*1 Corinthians 10:6-13* (2)*Romans 1:27-32* (3)*2 Timothy 2:22* (4)*1 Peter 2:11* (5)*Psalms 119:11* (6)*1 John 2:16,17* (7)*Matthew 6:33* (8)*Titus 2:12,13* (9)*Romans 8:1-14* (10)*John 16:33* **Other Scriptures:** *Proverbs 6:25, Matthew 5:28, Romans 7:7, Galatians 5:16, 2 Peter 2:18, 3:3*

53

Renewing the Mind

Key Thought: God is renewing your mind through His Word.

Key Scripture: *"And do not be conformed to this world, but be transformed by the renewing of your mind, that you may prove what is that good and acceptable and perfect will of God"* (Rom. 12:2, NKJV).

Prayer: Thank you, Lord, for searching my heart and for understanding the thoughts of my imagination. As I seek you with all my heart, I find you,[1] and you enable me to bring every thought into captivity to obey you.[2] Your Word is a discerner of my thoughts and the intents of my heart.[3]

Dear heavenly Father, thank you for renewing my mind[4] through your Word. Your Word is true.[5] And your truth will set me free from worldly thinking.[6] I know that my natural ways are not your ways and my natural thoughts are not your thoughts.[7]

Because Jesus is my Lord, I am now a new creation,[8] made over in your image and likeness through the supernatural process of your salvation which came through truth[9] and grace.[10] Daily I *put off* the old man and *put on* the new man, that is renewed in knowledge after your image.[11]

By faith I walk in the Spirit. I am seated in heavenly places in Christ,[12] where I can see the world as you see it. My affections are now set on things above, not on things on the earth.[13] I look not at the things which are seen, but at the things which are not seen, for the things which are seen are temporal; but the things which are not seen are eternal.[14] As I do this, Lord, I know that my mind is being renewed to have your perspective.

Through the eyes of faith, I see substance given to all those things for which your Word gives me hope and I have solid evidence of all the good treasures of your kingdom, even though they are not yet all manifest in my life. I rejoice in the hope of all that is yet to come.[15] For this cause I faint not, even though the outward man may perish, because the inward man is being renewed day by day.[16]

Thank you for the renewing process that is taking place in the spirit of my mind as I put on the new man, which after God is created in righteousness and true holiness.[17]

Lord, I determine now that I will set my mind on things that are true, honest, pure, lovely, of good report; on things that are excellent and praiseworthy. I will think on these things, knowing your peace will be with me.[18]

Continue to renew my mind, Lord, and I thank you for giving me grace to cooperate with you fully in the process of renewal and transformation.

References: *(1)1 Chronicles 28:9 (2)Proverbs 16:3 (3)Hebrews 4:12 (4)Romans 12:1,2 (5)John 17:17 (6)John 8:32 (7)Isaiah 55:8 (8)2 Corinthians 5:17 (9)John 1:7 (10)Titus 2:11 (11)Colossians 3:9,10 (12)Ephesians 2:6 (13)Colossians 3:2 (14)2 Corinthians 4:18 (15)Hebrews 11:1 (16)2 Corinthians 4:16 (17)Ephesians 4:23,24 (18)Philippians 4:8* **Other Scriptures:** *Psalms 51:10, Matthew 12:25, 1 Corinthians 3:20, 1 John 2:15-17*

54

Freedom From a Negative Self-Concept

Key thought: I am fearfully and wonderfully made.

Key Scripture: *"I will praise thee; for I am fearfully and wonderfully made: marvelous are thy works; and that my soul knoweth right well. My substance was not hid from thee, when I was made in secret, and curiously wrought in the lowest parts of the earth. Thine eyes did see my substance, yet being unperfect; and in thy book all my members were written, which in continuance were fashioned, when as yet there was none of them"* (Ps. 139:14-16).

Prayer: Father, I thank you for your love which is from everlasting to everlasting. There is, therefore, no condemnation to me if I walk after your Spirit and not after my flesh.[1] Nothing can separate me from your love,[2] except my own refusal to receive it.

Help me to grow in your grace and knowledge, to see myself as you see me — complete in Jesus Christ. I thank you that you created me in your image[3] and that Jesus died for me to set me free from all negative powers.

When I became a Christian, Lord, I became a completely new creature in you. You transformed me into a wonderful, new creation of your handiwork. The old things are behind me now, and you have made all things new in my life.[4]

You have delivered me from the power of darkness and have translated me into your kingdom. Thank you, Lord. I am made complete in you; you are the head of all principality and power.[5]

I have put off the old man (including the negative way I used to view myself) and I have put on the new man which is renewed in knowledge after your image, Lord.[6] Thank you for changing me and helping me to love myself as you love me.

It is my desire, Lord, to stand perfect and complete in your will.[7] Thank you for showing me that your strength is made perfect in my weakness;[8] that I do not have to make myself perfect, but you are perfecting me.

O Lord, I am clay in your hands and you are the Potter. I am the work of your hands. You are the Lord and beside you there is no other. You have created the entire universe, Lord, and you are raising me up in righteousness.[9] You will direct me in all my ways.[10]

Thank you for shaping my life, Father. I am your workmanship, created in Christ Jesus unto good works, which you have before ordained that I should walk in them.[11] I am confident that you who have begun a good work in me will perform it until the day of Jesus Christ.[12] Praise you, Father.

References: (1)Romans 8:1 (2)Romans 8:38,39 (3)Genesis 1:26
(4)2 Corinthians 5:17 (5)Colossians 2:10 (6)Colossians 3:10
(7)Colossians 4:12 (8)2 Corinthians 12:9 (9)Isaiah 45:5-14
(10)Proverbs 3:6 (11)Ephesians 2:10 (12)Philippians 1:6
Other Scriptures: Psalms 103:17, Isaiah 64:9

55
Freedom From Rejection

Key Thought: Jesus never fails.

Key Scripture: *"Blessed are they which are persecuted for righteousness' sake: for theirs is the kingdom of heaven. Blessed are ye, when men shall revile you, and persecute you, and shall say all manner of evil against you falsely, for my sake. Rejoice, and be exceeding glad: for great is your reward in heaven"* (Matt. 5:10-12).

Prayer: Lord Jesus, you understand what rejection feels like. You were betrayed,[1] forsaken,[2] mocked, scorned and persecuted.[3] Thank you for assuring me that you will never leave me nor forsake me.[4] Even if others turn against me, you are always there.

You, Lord Jesus, were despised and rejected of men: a man of sorrows, and acquainted with grief.[5] You have borne my grief and carried my sorrows.[6] Thank you for lifting the pain of rejection from me.

The rejection I have experienced from _____ _____ causes me hurt and anguish, but I know this is not your will for me. By faith and an act of my will, in obedience to your Word, I choose to forgive _____ _____ for the pain and hurt his/her words and actions have brought to me. I receive your healing, Lord, and I pray for _____, that you will bless him/her with a knowledge of your will in all things.

I possess the treasure of your love and truth in the earthen vessel of my body. I know that the excellency of the power to overcome rejection is of you, Lord. I am troubled but not distressed. I am perplexed but not in despair. I am persecuted, but not forsaken. I am cast down, but not destroyed. Praise God! Your life, Lord Jesus, is being made manifest in my body and my outlook.[7]

Teach me your way, O Lord, and lead me in a plain path, because of my enemies.[8] Your face, Lord, will I seek. When loved ones forsake me, then you will take me up.[9] As I wait on you I take courage. You are strengthening my heart. Thank you, Lord.

You, Lord, are my helper. I will not fear what men may do to me. Wonderful Jesus, you are the same yesterday, and today, and forever.[4] I trust in your promise that you will always be with me.

References: (1) *Mark 14:44* (2)*Mark 14:50* (3)*Mark 15:16-20*
(4)*Hebrews 13:5-8* (5)*Isaiah 53:3* (6)*Mark 15:34*
(7)*2 Corinthians 4:7-10* (8)*Psalms 27:11* (9)*Psalms 27:9,10*
Other Scriptures: Ezra 9:9

56
Conquering the Thought Life

Key Thought: Right thinking leads to right acting.

Key Scripture: *"For my thoughts are not your thoughts, neither are your ways my ways, saith the Lord. For as the heavens are higher than the earth, so are my ways higher than your ways, and my thoughts than your thoughts"* (Isa. 55:8,9).

Prayer: Help me, Lord, to line my thoughts up with yours. You know my thoughts and I am aware that some of the imaginations, or thoughts, of the human heart are evil,[1] so I humbly ask you to help me control my thought life.

Remove all vanity from my thinking, Lord,[2] and replace it with the wonderful comfort that comes from your Holy Spirit.[3] I hate vain thoughts, Lord, but I love your Word.[4] Teach me to apply my heart to wisdom[5] and to behold wondrous things from your Word. I will meditate on your Word day and night.[6]

Search me, O God, and know my heart; try me, and know my thoughts, and see if there be any wicked way in me, and lead me in the way everlasting.[7] The thoughts of the righteous are right,[8] and I want your righteousness to invade my thought life.

I commit my works unto you, O Lord, knowing that, in doing so, my thoughts will be established.[9] You have shown me that the thoughts of the diligent lead to abundant living.[10] Thank you, Lord.

Make me aware of areas of wrong thinking in my mind. Thank you, Father. I repent of these specific thoughts: _____, and I willingly bring them into the captivity of obedience to you, Lord.[11] No longer may they have any power over me. Praise God!

Your Word pierces to the dividing asunder of soul and spirit, and of the joints and marrow. Thank you for your Word that discerns the thoughts and intents of my heart.[12] Help me to respond to its wisdom in all my thinking, Lord, as I submit my thought life to you. Let your mind be in me, Lord Jesus.[13]

References: (1)Genesis 6:5 (2)Psalms 94:11 (3)John 14:26 (4)Psalms 119:113 (5)Psalms 90:12 (6)Psalms 1:2 (7)Psalms 139:23,24 (8)Proverbs 12:5 (9)Proverbs 16:3 (10)Proverbs 21:5 (11)2 Corinthians 10:5 (12)Hebrews 4:12 (13)Philippians 2:5 **Other Scriptures:** 1 Chronicles 28:9, Proverbs 16:3, Matthew 15:19, 1 Corinthians 3:20

57

Freedom From Worry

Key Thought: You don't have to worry.

Key Scripture: *"And we know that all things work together for good to them that love God, to them who are the called according to his purpose"* (Rom. 8:28).

Prayer: Heavenly Father, because I know you care for me I also know that I can cast all my cares upon you.[1] Forgive me for worrying; I know I don't have to bear my burdens alone. Thank you for inviting me to come unto you and for your wonderful promise of rest.[2] I receive your rest as I lay my burdens of worry down.

When I look at my life as I know I should, I realize I have no reason for worry whatsoever. Nothing shall be able to separate me from the love of God which is in Christ Jesus our Lord — not things past nor present, nor things yet to come.[3] Thank you, Jesus, for reassuring me that you are working your purposes out in my life and that you are the Master of circumstances. You have promised to supply all my needs.[4]

There is no fear in your love because your perfect love casts out all fear.[5] You have told us, Father, not to fear because it is your good pleasure to give us the Kingdom.[6] I resolve never to lose sight of the precious promises of your Word.

Lord, you have commanded me not to worry about anything. Instead, you want me to spend my time in prayer and supplication and to let my requests be known unto you with thanksgiving.[7] Lord, how thankful I am that you have provided prayer and praise as practical outlets to prevent us from worry.

I will take no thought for tomorrow, for tomorrow will take care of itself. I will take one day at a time, Lord, because you have shown me that this day's trouble is enough for one day.[8]

Standing on the promises of your Word, therefore, I come unto you now. Lord Jesus, I receive your love as I pray, and I place all my worries and cares in your hands, knowing fully that you take care of everything that is given to you.[9] Thank you for caring about me so much. I love you, Lord.

References: (1)1 Peter 5:7 (2)Matthew 11:28 (3)Romans 8:38,39 (4)Philippians 4:19 (5)1 John 4:18 (6)Luke 12:32 (7)Philippians 4:6,7 (8)Matthew 6:34 (9)2 Timothy 1:12
Other Scriptures: Psalms 37:8, Mark 4:19, Luke 21:34, Galatians 5:1, Hebrews 4:16

SPIRITUAL GROWTH

58

Walking in God's Fulness

Key Thought: God is able to do much more that we ask or think.

Key Scripture: *"For it is God who works in you both to will and to do for His good pleasure"* (Philippians 2:13, NKJV).

Prayer: I bow my knees to you, God, the Father of my/our Lord Jesus Christ, of whom the whole family in heaven and earth is named, that you would grant me/us, according to the riches of your glory, to be strengthened with might by your Spirit in the inner man, that Christ may dwell in my/our heart(s) by faith; and that I/we, being rooted and grounded in love, may be able to comprehend with all saints what is the breadth, and length, and depth and height; and to know (and experience) the love of Christ, which passes knowledge, that I/we may be filled with all your fulness. Now unto you who are able to do exceedingly abundantly above all that I/we ask or think, according to the power that works in me/us, unto you, O God, be glory in the church by Christ Jesus throughout all ages, world without end. Amen.[1]

References: (1)*Ephesians 3:14-21.*

59

Walking in Holiness

Key Thought: God's standard is holiness.

Key Scripture: *"Follow peace with all men, and holiness, without which no man shall see the Lord"* (Heb. 12:14).

Prayer: Thank you, Father, for your righteousness which enables me to walk in holiness before you. Therefore, by your mercies, O God, I now present my body a living sacrifice, holy, acceptable unto you, which is my reasonable service.[1]

Lord, I give unto you the glory that is due your name. I would come before you and worship you in the beauty of holiness.[2] I repent of my sins and ask you to bring me into holiness without which I cannot see you.

I desire to be holy as you are holy, Lord.[3] Impart your holiness to me so that I might be pure in heart, capable of seeing you as you are, in all your holiness, honor, power and majesty. Holy is your name, Father.

Let me serve you with pureness of heart. Thank you, Jesus, for being the Son of God with power, according to the Spirit of holiness, by the resurrection from the dead.[4] You, Lord, have given me the grace to be holy. Thank you.

You are renewing me, Lord, in the spirit of my mind. Because of this, I am able to put on the new man, which after God is created in righteousness and true holiness.[5] From this point on, I will continue in faith and love and holiness, with self-control.[6]

Thank you, Father, for your chastening that makes it possible for me to partake of your holiness. Help me to realize that I learn obedience through your correction. Thank you for the peaceable fruit of righteousness which comes through your chastisement.[7]

Your promises are splendid, Father. Your Word is a power-packed book of promises. Realizing your wonderful promises, I cleanse myself from all filthiness of the flesh and spirit, perfecting holiness in the fear of you.[8]

You, Lord, are holy. You sit upon your throne, high and lifted up, and your train fills the Temple. I join with the angels who cry, "Holy, holy, holy, is the Lord of hosts: the whole earth is filled with your glory."[9] Help me to see you in all your holiness, Lord, and in so seeing you, to desire to be holy as you are holy.[3]

References: (1)*Romans 12:1,2* (2)*1 Chronicles 16:29* (3)*Leviticus 19:2* (4)*Romans 1:4* (5)*Ephesians 4:24* (6)*1 Timothy 2:15, NKJV* (7)*Hebrews 12:10,11* (8)*2 Corinthians 7:1* (9)*Isaiah 6:1-3* **Other Scriptures:** *Leviticus 20:7, 2 Chronicles 31:18,21, 1 Thessalonians 3:13*

60
Walking in the Light

Key Thought: God is light; in Him there is no darkness.

Key Scripture: *"But if we walk in the light, as he is in the light, we have fellowship one with another, and the blood of Jesus Christ, his Son, cleanseth us from all sin"* *(1 John 1:7).*

Prayer: Lord God, your Word is a lamp unto my feet and a light unto my path.[1] Teach me to walk in the light of your Word in the same way you walk in the light.[2] Your light reveals my needs and your salvation, and when I see those needs in the light of your grace and power and righteousness I have faith that you will undertake to meet my needs and fulfill your salvation in me.

You are my light and my salvation; whom shall I fear? You are the strength of my life; of whom shall I be afraid?[3] These facts give me great confidence.

Lord, you have sent out your light and truth. Let them lead me; let them bring me to your holy hill, and to your tabernacles. Then will I go unto the altar of God, unto God who is my exceeding joy. Then will I praise you, O God, my God.[4] Your light brightens my life and purifies my soul.

It is true that the people who know your joyful sound will walk in the light of your countenance, O Lord. In your name I will rejoice all day, and in your righteousness I will be exalted for you are the glory of my strength: you are my defense.[5]

Thank you, Father, for delivering me from the power of darkness and for translating me into the kingdom of your dear Son in whom I have redemption through His blood, even the forgiveness of my sins.[6] Glory to God!

I will look unto you, Lord; I will wait for you who are the God of my salvation: I know you will hear me. I rejoice in you, O Lord, because I know that when I fall I will arise; when I sit in darkness, you will be a light unto me.[7]

Lord Jesus, in you is life, and that life is the light of men. Your light has shone in the darkness, and the darkness cannot overcome it. Keep me walking in your light, Lord, because you are the true light that lights every man who comes into the world.[8] The light of your life and your Word gives me the direction and wisdom I need.

References: (1)*Psalms 119:105* (2)*1 John 1:7* (3)*Psalms 27:1-3* (4)*Psalms 43:3,4* (5)*Psalms 89:15-18* (6)*Colossians 1:13,14* (7)*Micah 7:7,8* (8)*John 1:4-9* **Other Scriptures:** *Matthew 4:16, Matthew 5:14, Romans 13:12, Ephesians 5:8*

61

Walking in Revelation

Key Thought: God loves to give wisdom and revelation to His children.

Key Scripture: *"Now we have received, not the spirit of the world, but the spirit who is from God, that we might know the things that have been freely given to us by God"* *(1 Corinthians 2:12, NKJV).*

Prayer: God of my Lord Jesus Christ, the Father of Glory, I/we pray that you would give me/us the spirit of wisdom and revelation in the knowledge of you, the eyes of my/our understanding being enlightened; that I/we may know (and understand) the hope of your calling and what are the riches of the glory of your inheritance in the saints, and that I/we may know what is the exceeding greatness of your power toward me/us who believe(s), according to the working of your mighty power, which you wrought in Christ when you raised Him from the dead, and set Him at your own right hand in the heavenly places, far above all principality, and power, and might, and dominion, and every name that is named, not only in this world, but also in that which is to come. And you put all things under His feet and gave Him to be the head over all things to the church, which is His body, the fulness of Him which filleth all in all. Amen.[1]

References: (1)Ephesians 1:17-23

62

Tithes and Offerings

Key Thought: Everything we own belongs to God.

Key Scripture: *"Will a man rob God? Yet ye have robbed me. But ye say, Wherein have we robbed thee? In tithes and offerings...Bring ye all the tithes into the storehouse, that there may be meat in mine house, and prove me now herewith, saith the Lord of hosts, if I will not open you the windows of heaven, and pour you out a blessing, that there shall not be room enough to receive it" (Mal. 3:8-10).*

Prayer: Lord, I realize that all I have comes from you. Help me always to remember to return the firstfruits to you.[1] You command the giving of tithes, Lord, as an act of obedience and an avenue of blessing.[2] According as I purpose in my heart, so let me give both tithes and offerings. Holy Spirit, rule all the purposing of my heart. I purpose in my heart to give tithes and offerings to you regularly, Lord, and to give cheerfully, never grudgingly.[3]

It is my desire to lay up treasures in heaven where moth and rust cannot corrupt them and no thief can steal them[4]. I repent now, Lord, of all selfishness that would prevent me from giving freely.

Direct me in all my giving, Lord. Help me to place my tithes and offerings in the place of your choosing. I know that my giving is an act of worship to you, Lord, and what a privilege it is. I rejoice in the act of giving because of all the good things you have given to me, Lord.

Bless my giving, Lord. May my tithes and offerings be used to build your kingdom on earth as it is in heaven. Blessed be the most high God[5] who has delivered me from all my enemies and enabled me to give. I will always remember that it is you, Lord, who gives me the power to obtain wealth in order that your covenant may be fulfilled.[6] Help me never to consume upon my own lusts that which you have given to me to forward the work of the kingdom and help those in need.[7]

Love always gives, Lord. You loved the world so much that you gave your only Son.[8] I love you with all my heart, soul, mind and strength and I will delight to give to your work. When I see the needs of those around me, I will respond by giving as unto you.

As I give cheerfully and generously, I know I will receive good measure, pressed down, and shaken together, and running over. Help me to remember that the same measure I give out will be measured back to me.[9] I realize, Lord, that only what I give away will I be able to keep for all eternity. Trusting fully in your promises, Lord, I can freely give and freely receive.[10] I know that you will supply all of my needs according to your riches in glory by Christ Jesus. I thank you, Father, in Jesus' name.[11]

References: (1)Deuteronomy 26 (2)Malachi 3:8-10
(3)2 Corinthians 9:7 (4)Matthew 6:19,20 (5)Daniel 4:34
(6)Deuteronomy 8:18 (7)James 4:3 (8)John 3:16 (9)Luke 6:38
(10)Matthew 10:8 (11)Philippians 4:19 *Other Scriptures:*
Genesis 14:20, Numbers 18:28, Nehemiah 12:44, Luke 18:12,
Ephesians 2:4

63

Walking in Truth

Key Thought: Jesus Christ is the way, the truth and the life.

Key Scripture: *"He that speaketh truth sheweth forth righteousness: but a false witness deceit" (Prov. 12:17).*

Prayer: God of truth and light, I come to you now seeking truth in the inward parts of my life because I know that is what you want.[1] Fill me with your truth, Lord, as I grow more acquainted with your Word of truth. Lead me in your truth,[2] bring to my remembrance all the things that Jesus taught, and help me to walk in the freedom that truth always brings. I know your truth, Lord, and your truth has set me free.[3]

Teach me your way, O Lord, that I might walk in your truth.[4] I choose the way of truth,[5] and I want to learn to speak the truth in love to all.[6] This paves the way for me to grow up in you, Lord, in all things.

My mouth shall speak truth; wickedness is an abomination to my lips. Thank you for showing me that it is by mercy and truth that iniquity is purged.[7] As you reveal your truth to me, Father, give me grace to walk in it so that I will always depart from evil.

Lord Jesus, you are the incarnate Word of God, and you are full of grace and truth. Fill my life, Lord, that your grace, mercy and truth will flow naturally from me in all that I say and do. He that does truth comes to the light, that his deeds may be manifest, that they are wrought in God.[8] May others see your truth in my life.

Master, you prayed that your children would be sanctified through your Word of truth. I receive your truth and its sanctifying work in my life. As the Father sent you into the world, so are you sending me.[9] What a privilege and joy it is to be able to serve you in the truth and power of the gospel.

Help me rightly to divide the Word of truth so that I might never be ashamed in your service and that I might be approved by you.[10] I accept your purification of my soul in obeying the truth through the Holy Spirit. As a result, I have been set free to love the brethren with unfeigned love, fervently and with a pure heart.[11] Thank you, Jesus.

References: (1)*Psalms 51:6* (2)*Psalms 25:5* (3)*John 8:32* (4)*Psalms 86:11* (5)*Psalms 119:30* (6)*Ephesians 4:15* (7)*Proverbs 16:6,7* (8)*John 3:21* (9)*John 17:17,18* (10)*2 Timothy 2:15* (11)*1 Peter 1:22* **Other Scriptures:** *Psalms 119:43, Proverbs 8:7, John 1:4*

64

Walking in Wisdom

Key Thought: The fear of the Lord is the beginning of wisdom.

Key Scripture: *"If any of you lacks wisdom, let him ask of God, that giveth to all men liberally, and upbraideth not; and it shall be given him"* (James 1:5).

Prayer: Thank you for your Word, Father, for it gives knowledge, instruction, wisdom, and understanding to all who pay attention to its truths. You promise to impart wisdom to me if I will listen to your words and attain unto your wise counsels. I enter your presence with trust, knowing that you will give me wisdom.[1]

Your wisdom is first pure; then peaceable, gentle, and easy to be entreated, full of mercy and good fruits, without partiality, and without hypocrisy. Thank you, Father, that your wisdom is so different from that of the world.[2]

Fill me with the spirit of wisdom that I might discern your will.[3] With you, Lord, there is strength and wisdom.[4] Let my mouth speak wisdom, Lord, because of the righteousness you have imparted to me.[5] In the hidden parts of my life, make me to know wisdom.[6] Teach me to number my days, Lord, that I will always apply my heart unto wisdom.[7]

I ask you to fill me with the knowledge of your will in all wisdom and spiritual understandings. This will enable me to walk worthy of you, Lord, unto all pleasing and to be fruitful in every good work, increasing in the knowledge of your ways.[8] Thank you for this promise of wisdom, Lord.

Your wisdom makes me happy, Lord, because the gain of it is better than fine gold. By wisdom you founded the earth and by knowledge you established the heavens.[9]

Lord Jesus, you are the wisdom and power of God. Because I am in you — and desire always to abide in you — you are made unto me wisdom, and righteousness, sanctification and redemption. It is this reality that causes me to glory in you forever.[10]

References: *(1)2 Chronicles 1:10 (2)James 3:15-17 (3)Exodus 28:3 (4)Job 12:13 (5)Psalms 37:30 (6)Psalms 51:6 (7)Psalms 90:12 (8)Colossians 1:9-11 (9)Proverbs 3:13-20 (10)1 Corinthians 1:22-31* **Other Scriptures:** *Genesis 12:1-2, Job 28:28, Psalms 32:8,9, Proverbs 2:6,7, Proverbs 4:7, Proverbs 16:3, Ecclesiastes 7:12, Acts 6:3, Romans 11:33, Colossians 2:3*

HEALTH AND HAPPINESS

65

Freedom From Financial Pressures

Key Thought: God owns the cattle on a thousand hills.

Key Scripture: *"Bring ye all the tithes into the storehouse, that there may be meat in mine house, and prove me now herewith, saith the Lord of hosts, if I will not open you the windows of heaven, and pour you out a blessing, that there shall not be room enough to receive it"* (Mal. 3:10).

Prayer: Heavenly Father, you are greater than I can possibly imagine and greatly to be praised.[1] I praise you for your goodness and faithfulness to me. I know you desire to bless me more than I can realize, but I also know the key to that blessing is to be found in obedience to the teachings of your Word. Help me to obey you in the area of my finances, Lord, so that I might become a good steward over all you've given to me.

Father, help me to understand that in your economy, resources are meant to flow freely from the place of excess to the place of need.[2] Lord, you give power to obtain wealth for a purpose — that you may establish your covenant of salvation through me.[3]

I choose to believe your Word, Lord, and I believe that as I obey you with my tithes and offerings you will mercifully fulfill your promises and open the windows of heaven and pour your blessings forth abundantly to me. I believe also that you will prevent the enemy from devouring my finances and I will be called blessed by those who see your goodness to me.

I choose to give out of a heart of love and obedience, knowing it is more blessed to give than to receive.[4] Yet I know, Lord, that as I give, it will be given to me good measure pressed down and running over. For with the same measure that I give it will be given to me.[5] This is your plan, Lord, and I willingly honor it with cheerful giving as you supply, for you are able to make all grace abound toward me for every good work.[6]

You have commanded me not to owe any man anything except to love him.[7] Help me, Lord, to manage my financial resources better so that I will get out from under the load of debt[8] and be freed to serve you more fully and to give to the important causes of your kingdom.

Lord, godliness with contentment is great gain in my life. I brought nothing into this world and it is certain that I will take nothing out.[9] Therefore, let me learn to be content in whatsoever state I am.[10] Instead of seeking after the things of this world,[11] I want your righteousness, godliness, faith, love, patience and meekness. As I learn to seek you and your kingdom purposes *first,* along with your righteousness, all other things will be added unto me.[12]

The things that are seen, O Lord, are temporal, but the things that are unseen are eternal.[13] Help me to fix my focus on that which is eternal, and to lay up treasures in heaven where moth and rust cannot corrupt and the enemy cannot steal.[14] You are my Lord; I have been bought with the price of your shed blood; I am no longer my own, but all I am and have are yours.[15] Give me wisdom, Lord,[16] so that I will be able to get my finances in order under your Lordship.

References: (1)Psalms 48:1 (2)2 Corinthians 8:14
(3)Deuteronomy 8:18 (4)Acts 20:35 (5)Luke 6:38

(6)2 Corinthians 9:7,8 (7)Romans 13:8
(8)Proverbs 22:7 (9)1 Timothy 6:6-10 (10)Philippians 4:11-13
(11)Colossians 3:1,2 (12)Matthew 6:31-34 (13)2 Corinthians 4:18
(14)Matthew 6:19-21 (15)1 Corinthians 6:19,20 (16)James 1:5
Other Scriptures: *Colossians 3:23,24, 3 John 2*

66
Healing and Health

Key Thought: God loves to heal His children.

Key Scripture: *"A merry heart doeth good like a medicine: but a broken spirit drieth the bones" (Prov. 17:22).*

Prayer: Lord Jesus, you are the Great Physician. All healing comes from you. Thank you for caring so much about those who are ill. Thank you for your healing power.

Your Word says that healing is your children's bread.[1] It says you are the Lord that heals me. [2] And that by your stripes we are healed.[3]

That you took my infirmities and carried my sickness.[4] And whatever things I desire when I pray to believe I receive them and I shall have them.[5] Therefore, I receive your healing now, Lord, in my area of physical need of _____. I believe you are restoring me to health and vitality.

Your Scriptures declare that it is your will for your people to walk in health. Because I diligently hearken to your voice, and want to do what is right in your sight, you have promised that you will put none of these diseases upon me.[2] How I thank you for this promise, Lord.

Bless the Lord, O my soul, and forget not all His benefits.[6] You forgive all my iniquities and you heal all my diseases.[7] You have redeemed my life from destruction and you crown me with your lovingkindness and tender mercies.

You satisfy my mouth with good things so that my youth is renewed like the eagle's.[8]

It is so good to dwell in the secret place of the most high God, and to abide under your shadow. You are my refuge and my fortress — my God in whom I trust. You will deliver me from the noisome pestilence. Even though a thousand may fall by my side, and ten thousand at my right hand, it shall not come near me. No evil will befall me; neither shall any plague come near my dwelling. Thank you for giving your angels charge over me.[9]

You are the Lord who heals me.[2] You have sent your Word to heal me when I am sick.[10] Jesus, you healed everyone who came to you in faith, and the prayer of faith will save the sick and you will raise him up.[11] Thank you for healing me and enabling me to walk in health.

You heal the broken in heart and bind up all our wounds.[12] You are the Sun of righteousness who rises with healing in your wings.[13] You are the balm of Gilead.[14] I place all my hope in you, O God. I shall ever praise you because you are the health of my countenance, and my God.[15]

I love you, Lord. As my love for you flows forth in ministry to the oppressed and needy, you will cause my light to break forth as the morning and my health shall spring forth speedily. Your glory shall be my rear guard.[16] You have promised to restore health to me and to heal me of all wounds.[17] You are truly the Great Physician and the giver of all health. Thank you, Lord.

References: (1)Mark 7:27 (2)Exodus 15:26 (3)Isaiah 53:5 (4)Matthew 8:17 (5)Mark 11:24 (6)Psalms 103:2 (7)Psalms 103:3 (8)Psalms 103:4,5 (9)Psalms 91 (10)Psalms 107:20 (11)James 5:15,16 (12)Psalms 147:3 (13)Malachi 4:2 (14)Jeremiah 8:22 (15)Psalms 42:11 (16)Isaiah 58:8 (17)Jeremiah 30:17 *Other Scriptures:* Proverbs 3:8, Proverbs 16:24, 3 John 2

67

When All Looks Hopeless

Key Thought: Life with Christ is an endless hope.

Key Scripture: *"Now the God of hope fill you with all joy and peace in believing, that ye may abound in hope, through the power of the Holy Ghost" (Rom. 15:13).*

Prayer: God of all hope, I come to you now because I truly have nowhere else to turn. All appears hopeless, Lord, because of _____. Despite circumstances, however, I turn to you because your Word declares that Christ in me is the hope of glory.[1] Lord Jesus Christ, fill my life with your hope so that I might be able to glorify you in the midst of suffering and that I might be enabled by your Spirit to hope unto the end.

I know it is not your will for me to live in discouragement and despair. I recognize that my sense of hopelessness is the work of the enemy. Please forgive me for my lack of hope, Father. I renounce all hopelessness now and I replace it with the faith and hope your Word promises.

Help me to be like Abraham who believed in hope against all hope.[2] I know that the hope you are imparting to me, Father, will prevent me from being ashamed. You are filling me with your hope, joy, peace and faith so that I will abound in hope through the power of the Holy Spirit.[3] Thank you, Father.

I put on the breastplate of righteousness[4] and a right relationship with you, based on submission, trust and obedience. And for an helmet, I put on the hope of salvation.[5] Lord Jesus Christ, you love me with an everlasting love, and you have given me everlasting consolation and good hope through grace.[6] I receive your precious gifts in my life now, Lord.

I resolve to lay hold upon the hope you have set before me, Father. Your hope is the anchor of my soul and it is sure and steadfast.[7] I will hope continually, and I will yet praise you more and more.[8]

Thank you for the happiness that comes from trusting in you, Lord. You are my hope in the day of evil. I trust in you and hope in you because you are my Father and my God. You have promised *you* will never leave me nor forsake me.[9] You will always be with me. I take you at your Word, holy Father. I rejoice in you as you fill me with hope.

References: (1)Colossians 1:27 (2)Romans 4:18 (3)Romans 15:13 (4)Ephesians 6:15 (5)1 Thessalonians 5:8 (6)2 Thessalonians 2:16 (7)Hebrews 6:18,19 (8)Psalms 71:14 (9)Hebrews 13:5
Other Scriptures: Psalms 108:1, Zechariah 9:12, Romans 5:5, 2 Corinthians 3:12, 1 Peter 1:13

68

Deliverance From a Mental Disorder

Key Thought: God wants you to experience total wholeness.

Key Scripture: *"For God hath not given us the spirit of fear; but of power, and of love, and of a sound mind"* (2 Tim. 1:7).

Prayer: God, my Father, when the pressures of life threaten to overwhelm me, help me to remember that you want me to be every whit whole.[1] In Christ Jesus, you have provided a way for me to be free from depression, anxiety, guilt, worry and every mental disorder. You do not want me to be a victim of any of these things. Thank you, Lord, for your so complete salvation.

You do not want me to live with any mental disorder, Father. I beseech you to set me free, according to your lovingkindness. Lord Jesus, you are delivering me from the curse and torment of mental illness. You have promised to heal me. I do not have to be this way any longer. As I pray, I receive your healing deliverance that sets me free from the affliction of _____. I will not give in to its destructive power any longer for you have made me whole.

Faith in your name and your Word makes me strong. Perfect soundness in mind, soul and body comes through faith in you, Lord.[2] I have your mind within me, and this frees me from all mental disorders. Let your mind rule within me at all times.[3]

You are coming, Lord, and this confidence keeps me from being shaken in mind and being troubled in my spirit and mind. I gird up the loins of my mind in all sobriety, knowing that your grace is given to me by the revelation you have imparted through your Word.[4]

You have commanded me not to be troubled, but to believe in you. It is so easy to grow troubled in mind over so many things, Lord,[5] but your Word shows me that one thing is needful: to sit in your presence and to learn of you. Help me choose that good part which can never be taken away from me.[6]

When I grow troubled, and distressing thoughts arise from within my heart, help me draw near to you, for you are a very present help in time of trouble.[7] I will not let my heart be troubled because I believe in you.[8] You have given me supernatural peace.[9]

Thank you, Lord, for your provision of mental health.

References: (1)John 7:23 (2)Acts 3:16 (3)Philippians 2:5
(4)1 Peter 1:13 (5)2 Thessalonians 2:1,2 (6)Luke 10:41,42
(7)Psalms 46:1 (8)John 14:1,27 (9)Philippians 4:7
Other Scriptures: Matthew 24:6, Luke 4:18, 1 Corinthians 2:16,
1 Peter 3:14, 3 John 2

69

Daily Provision

Key Thought: My God is the God of more than enough.

Key Scripture: *"But my God shall supply all your need according to his riches in glory by Christ Jesus"* (Phil. 4:19).

Prayer: Heavenly Father, you never forsake the righteous. The seed of the righteous shall never have to beg for bread.[1] You always give me my daily bread[2] and you will never fail to supply all my needs according to your riches in glory by Christ Jesus, my Lord.[3] All of my spiritual, physical, financial, social and emotional needs are supplied in Christ.

How I praise you and thank you, Lord, for your rich blessings in my life. You clothe the lilies and the grass of the field. You feed the fowls of the air.[4] I know you will take care of me. You love me, Father, and I love you.

Lord, your Word declares that if I will trust in you and do good, I will dwell securely in the land and be fed. I delight myself in you, Lord, and I thrill to realize that you are giving me the desires of my heart. Hallelujah! I commit my way to you and I trust in you;[5] I know, therefore, that you will bring everything I need to fruition in my life.

Help me to remember that a man's life does not consist in the abundance of the things he possesses;[6] rather it consists in spiritual abundance. Thank you, Lord Jesus, that you came that I might have life, and that I might have it more abundantly. You are my Good Shepherd.[7] You love me, Lord, and I love you.

You, Lord Jesus, are able to do exceeding abundantly above all that I ask or think, according to the power that works in me.[8] Thank you, Lord.

Father, I thank you that you know what things I need before I ask you.[9] Thank you that you want to give me what I need and for your faithfulness in meeting my needs. I seek first your kingdom and your righteousness and all the things I need are added unto me.[4] I believe this, Lord, and trusting you I enter into your rest.[10]

Help me to learn the difference between wants and needs, and to be content with the certain knowledge that you will supply all my needs.[3]

You say that a good man, a righteous man, is ever merciful and lends to the needy.[11] The world is yours and the fullness thereof.[12] You own the cattle on a thousand hills[13] and the wealth in every mine.[14] You are El Shaddai, the God of more than enough. I offer unto you my thanksgiving and I forget not all of your benefits to me.[15] Praise you, Lord!

References: (1)Psalms 37:25 (2)Luke 11:3 (3)Philippians 4:19 (4)Matthew 6:26-34 (5)Psalms 37:3-5 (6)Luke 12:15 (7)John 10:10,11 (8)Ephesians 3:20 (9)Matthew 6:8,32 (10)Hebrews 4:1 (11)Psalms 37:26 (12)Psalms 24:1 (13)Psalms 50:10 (14)Haggai 2:8 (15)Psalms 103:2 Other Scriptures: 1 Corinthians 10:26

70

Peaceful Sleep

Key Thought: Sleep is a gift of God.

Key Scripture: *"Thou hast put gladness in my heart, more than in the time that their corn and their wine increased. I will both lay me down in peace, and sleep: for thou, Lord, only makest me dwell in safety"* (Ps. 4:7, 8).

Prayer: Lord, thank you for the wonderful gift of peaceful sleep. Deep, peaceful sleep is from you,[1] and in the night watches your dreams and visions speak to my heart.[2]

Unless you, Lord, build the house, they who build it labor in vain. Except you keep the city, the watchman wakes in vain.[3] Help me remember, Lord, when I am troubled or anxious, when circumstances seem to close in on me or I have more to do than I can cope with, that it is vain to rise up early, to sit up late, to eat the bread of sorrows, for you give your beloved sleep.[4] I do not have to worry or fret. When I rise up early let it be for the joy of meeting you.[5] If I sit up late let it be because your Spirit has called me to communion[6] — but not for worry or self-indulgence.

The sleep of a laboring man is sweet whether he eats little or much, but the abundance of the rich will not permit him to sleep, if his focus is on his possessions, because this stirs up worry which prevents one from sleeping peacefully.[7] Help me to labor faithfully in your vineyard, Lord, and also to get the natural exercise I need so that my body desires sleep.

May your commandments be life unto my soul and grace to my neck. Then I will be able to walk in my way safely and my foot will not stumble. When I lie down I will not be afraid. I will lie down and my sleep will be sweet because I trust in you, Lord.[8]

You have satisfied the weary soul and you have replenished every sorrowful heart. Thank you for taking my weariness from me and removing my sorrow from me.[9] I will lie down in peace and sleep; for you, Lord, alone, make me dwell in safety.[10] The sleep you give is sweet unto me.[11]

References: (1)1 Samuel 26:12 (2)Job 4:13 (3)Psalms 127:1 (4)Psalms 127:2 (5)Proverbs 8:17 (6)Psalms 4:3,4 (7)Ecclesiastes 5:12 (8)Proverbs 3:22-24 (9)Jeremiah 31:25 (10)Psalms 4:8 (11)Jeremiah 31:26

71
Being Equipped for Success

Key Thought: Success requires faithfulness in the little things.

Key Scripture: *"This book of the law shall not depart out of thy mouth; but thou shalt meditate therein day and night, that thou mayest observe to do according to all that is written therein: for then thou shalt make thy way prosperous, and then thou shalt have good success" (Josh. 1:8).*

Prayer: Lord, I believe it is your desire for me to walk in success. If I walk not in the counsel of the ungodly, but delight myself in your Word, I will be like a tree planted by the rivers of water, that brings forth fruit in due season. My leaf shall not wither, and whatsoever I do shall prosper.[1]

Lord, you love me and I love you. You preserve the faithful and plentifully reward your children. Because of your faithfulness and love, I possess good courage and my heart is strengthened.[2]

Let me learn to measure prosperity and success according to the standards of your Word instead of the standards of the world. I desire to be successful in your eyes, Lord.

Teach me to be faithful in all my responsibilities, Lord. Your Word teaches that a faithful person will abound with blessings[3] and good success. You are the vine, Lord, and I am one of your branches. I delight to abide in you and rejoice that you abide in me. Help me remember that abiding is the key to fruitfulness and success. Without you I can do nothing.[4]

It is my heartfelt desire to hear you say to me, "Well done, good and faithful servant: you have been faithful over a few things, I will make you ruler over many things: enter into the joy of your Lord."[5] I want to be your good and faithful servant, Lord.[6]

Help me fulfill your law, Lord, and realize that you measure successful living by whether I love you with all my heart, and my neighbor as myself.[7] I will endeavor to owe no man anything, but love, because I realize that he who loves another has fulfilled the law.[8]

As I am more able to see things from your perspective, Lord, I realize anew that true success comes from doing things your way. I surrender my life to you now, and I know that success will follow. Praise you, Lord.

References: (1)Psalms 1 (2)Psalms 31:23,24 (3)Proverbs 28:20 (4)John 15:4,5 (5)Matthew 25:21-23 (6)Luke 19:17 (7)Galatians 5:14 (8)Romans 13:8 Other Scriptures: Nehemiah 7:2

PRAYERS THAT PREVAIL

PART III
Ministry to Others

A. Helping Others

B. Prayers for Others

HELPING OTHERS

72

Caring for Others

Key Thought: God remembers our labors of love.

Key Scripture: *"Brethren, if a man be overtaken in a fault, ye which are spiritual, restore such an one in the spirit of meekness; considering thyself, lest thou also be tempted. Bear ye one another's burdens, and so fulfill the law of Christ" (Gal. 6:1-2).*

Prayer: Heavenly Father, help me to remember the words of Jesus who said that whoever would be the chief shall be the servant of all. He gave us the perfect example by coming not to be ministered unto but to minister, and He gave His life as a ransom for many.[1] Thank you, Jesus.

I thank you for the example of the Good Samaritan, Lord, who valued the need to care and show forth your love more highly than man-made restrictions and rules. He showed the kind of compassion and mercy you exhibit and seek when he stopped to care for the physical needs of the injured man.[2] Help me, Lord, to be a caring neighbor to others, wherever I encounter need.

Help me to see that caring for others leads to happiness. Lord, you said that the merciful would be blessed for showing mercy to others.[3] You have shown me how my care for others will help them receive your mercy and turn to you.

In showing care for others, help me to do it with cheerfulness, because I realize what a privilege it is to show mercy. Let my love be without hypocrisy at all times, Lord, so that I might always be kindly affectioned toward others in brotherly love. In honor, Lord, I want to learn how to prefer others, to distribute to the necessity of the saints and to be given to hospitality.[4]

May I do everything possible to prevent division in your body, Lord. Help me get involved in the mutual caring of your body; teach us all to have the same care one for another. When a member suffers, Lord, help me to suffer with him and be willing to minister to his needs,[5] as well as to pray for him.[6] Lord, I thank you for the special joy that comes from knowing when I care for even the least among your brethren, I have really done it unto you.[7]

Father, keep before my remembrance the promised reward for those who keep the fast you have chosen by caring for the needs of the oppressed, the hungry, the poor, naked and homeless and those who are my own flesh.[8]

Thank you for the power of your love, Father, that enables me to care for others.

References: *(1)Mark 10:44,45 (2)Luke 10:25-37 (3)Matthew 5:7 (4)Romans 12:8-13 (5)1 Corinthians 12:25-27 (6)James 5:16 (7)Matthew 25:34-40 (8)Isaiah 58:6-8 **Other Scriptures:** Matthew 8:15, 2 Corinthians 9:1*

73
Comforting Others

Key Thought: Compassion for others leads us to comfort them.

Key Scripture: *"Blessed be God, even the Father of our Lord Jesus Christ, the Father of mercies, and the God of all comfort; Who comforteth us in all our tribulation, that we may be able to comfort them which are in any trouble, by the comfort wherewith we ourselves are comforted of God" (2 Cor. 1:3-4).*

Prayer: God of all comfort, I come thanking you for the comfort you give in all tribulation and asking you to comfort others through me. Thank you for giving me great comfort in so many difficult situations in my life. Help me to share that same comfort with others.

You have commanded me to comfort your people, Lord,[1] and what a privilege that responsibility is. You have comforted me in the same way a mother comforts her child.[2] You have been compassionate toward me as a loving father.[3] Help me to show tender, loving comfort to others.

You tell us those who mourn will be comforted and this will bring them blessedness.[4] Help me comfort those around me who mourn, and have suffered loss.[5] When grief and mourning come to me, Lord, help me remember to turn to you for the comfort I will need. Thank you, Lord, that you give beauty for ashes, the oil of joy for mourning, and the garment of praise for the spirit of heaviness. May I always glorify you by receiving your comfort.[6]

Thank you for giving me salvation through Jesus Christ. Thank you for dying for us, Lord, so that whether we wake or sleep, we will be able to live together with you.

You promised you would not leave us comfortless. You sent the Comforter (your Holy Spirit) to abide with us.[7] Thank you, Lord. May the Spirit of comfort so fill my life that others will find your comfort through me.

*References: (1)Isaiah 40:1 (2)Isaiah 66:13 (3)Psalms 103:13 (4)Matthew 5:4 (5)1 Thessalonians 4:18 (6)Isaiah 61:3 (7)John 14:16-18 **Other Scriptures:** 1 Thessalonians 5:11*

74
Encouraging Others

Key Thought: Encouragement imparts courage.

Key Scripture: *"And he gave some, apostles; and some, prophets; and some, evangelists, and some, pastors and teachers; For the perfecting of the saints, for the work of the ministry, for the edifying of the body of Christ: Till we all come in the unity of the faith, and of the knowledge of the Son of God, unto a perfect man, unto the measure of the stature of the fullness of Christ"* (Eph. 4:11-13).

Prayer: Lord, I thank you for your encouragement in my life. Help me always to share it with others. Like David, I want to encourage myself in you, my God.[1] Only then, I realize, will I be able to encourage others.

Teach me how to build others up, to encourage them in the precious faith you've imparted to us. It is your will, Father, for those of us who are strong in you to bear the infirmities of the weak and not to please ourselves. Let me encourage my neighbor in this way, for his good, to build him up.[2]

As you fill me with your Spirit, I will speak encouragement, edification and comfort to others.[3] Help me always to remember that the gifts and power you have imparted to me, Lord, are to be used to help and encourage and edify others. May I never use them selfishly or destructively. I know it is your love alone that makes this possible; your love always edifies and strengthens.[4]

Let me show others how to be of good cheer, Lord, for you have overcome the world. Even though we have tribulation in the world; in you, Lord, we have peace.[5] Help me share your peace with others.

It is my goal, Lord, to follow after the things that make for peace, and things wherewith I will be able to edify and encourage others.[6] May your people always be encouraged by what I say and do. Let my words always edify and minister grace,[7] and let my life be an encouragement at all times.

When a fellow-believer is discouraged, prompt me, Lord, and enable me to speak a word in season to him.[8] Help me to comfort others with the same comfort I've received from you.[9]

References: (1)1 Samuel 30:6 (2)Romans 15:1-2 (3)1 Corinthians 14:3 (4)1 Corinthians 14:26 (5)John 16:33 (6)Romans 14:19 (7)Ephesians 4:29 (8)Proverbs 15:23 (9)2 Corinthians 1:4 **Other Scriptures:** *1 Corinthians 8:1, Ephesians 4:12-16, 1 Thessalonians 5:11*

75
Sharing the Faith

Key Thought: The greatest of all gifts is in your hands to give.

Key Scripture: *Go ye therefore, and teach all nations, baptizing them in the name of the Father, and of the Son, and of the Holy Ghost: Teaching them to observe all things whatsoever I have commanded you: and, lo, I am with you alway, even unto the end of the world" (Matt. 28:19-20).*

Prayer: Heavenly Father, thank you for sending the Holy Spirit to empower me to do the work you have called me to do. Because of His power, I am able to be your witness wherever I go.[1] Help me to be faithful to that important calling.

I am so happy, Lord, to be able to declare the glad tidings of Jesus to all with whom I come in contact.[2] May I be like the servant who went forth, into the highways and hedges, to invite people to the feast.[3] So empower me, Lord, I pray, that others will see the truth of your life in me and will want to taste and see that you are good.[4]

I repent of each time that I've failed to share the faith with people who need to know you. May I never again let any such opportunity go by without giving a witness to your saving grace.

Lord Jesus, your attitude reflects compassion on the lost at every opportunity. I want to be like you by going after those who are lost with zeal and compassion. I will declare what I have seen and heard to others so they will be able to have fellowship with you and with your people.[5] Thank you, Lord, for the joy this brings.

Thank you for the fruit of the righteous which is a tree of life. Let me share that fruit with others, fully realizing, Lord, that he who wins souls is wise.[6] Fill me with your wisdom.[7]

I want to be like many servants in your Word who always put you first, and determined in their hearts to declare your truth to all.[8] Let me invite each person to come to you as I declare to others what you have done for my soul.[9]

Thank you for letting me be a part of your army, Lord, commissioned to go forth in your name, declaring your glory among the heathen and your wonders among all people.[10] Thank you, too, for appointing me as your ambassador of reconciliation to encourage others to be reconciled with God and become citizens of the Kingdom of heaven. Help me represent you just as if you were representing yourself.[11] I want to be your faithful witness, Lord.

References: (1)Acts 1:8 (2)Acts 13:32 (3)Luke 14:21-23
(4)Psalms 34:8 (5)1 John 1:2 (6)Proverbs 11:30 (7)James 3:17
(8)Job 15:17 (9)Psalms 66:16 (10)Psalms 96:3
(11)2 Corinthians 5:20 **Other Scriptures:** Luke 15:4

76

Walking in Friendship

Key Thought: Friendship requires openness.

Key Scripture: *"A man that hath friends must shew himself friendly; and there is a friend that sticketh closer than a brother" (Prov. 18:24).*

Prayer: Lord Jesus, you have shown us the importance of friendship. You exhibited the caring and support that a friend should always have in your relationship with others.

Teach me to pray for my friends. When Job prayed for his friends, you turned his captivity. The end result was that Job received (from your hands) twice as much as he had before[1].

You have commanded me to love others as you have loved me, Lord. There is no greater love than the love you demonstrated by laying down your life for your friends.[2] May I be willing to die, if need be, for my friends. But, more important, help me be willing to lay down my life daily for the people you love, so that, in my servant spirit, they may see you.

May I never do anything through strife or vainglory, Lord. In lowliness of mind may I esteem others better than myself. Let me not be preoccupied with my own needs, Father. Help me focus on the needs of others.[3]

Thank you for allowing me to be your friend, Lord Jesus. Help me to remember that this special friendship requires me to do whatever you command. Thank you for the intimate friendship with you which permits me to learn all the things the Father has shared with you.[2]

Keep me unspotted from the world, Lord.[4] I know that friendship with the world is enmity with you.[5] I do not want to be your enemy; I want to be your friend.

A true friend loves at all times. Help me become that kind of friend to the people you bring to me, remembering always that a brother is born for the day of adversity.[6]

When I feel friendless, please remind me that you are my friend and that you are a friend who will always be closer than a brother. Help me to remember that in order to have friends, first I must be friendly. I will reach out to others in your love, Lord.[7]

When a friend rebukes me openly, let me hear what you are saying to me through him. The wounds of a true friend are faithful.[8] Lord, like Abraham, I desire to be known as the friend of God.[9]

References: (1)Job 42:10 (2)John 15:12-17 (3)Philippians 2:3,4 (4)James 1:27 (5)James 4:4 (6)Proverbs 17:17 (7)Proverbs 18:24 (8)Proverbs 27:6 (9)James 2:23

77

Walking in Mercy

Key Thought: The mercies of the Lord endure forever.

Key Scripture: *"He hath shewed thee, O man, what is good; and what doth the Lord require of thee, but to do justly, and to love mercy, and to walk humbly with thy God?" (Mic. 6:8)*

Prayer: Thank you, Father, for your mercy and grace. I bless you, Lord, because you redeemed my life from destruction and crowned me with your lovingkindness and your tender mercies. You are merciful and gracious, slow to anger, and plenteous in mercy.[1] Your lovingkindness is better than life to me.[2]

It is by your mercies, Lord, that we are not consumed by the evils around us. Thank you that your compassion never fails. Your mercies are new every morning, and great is your faithfulness. You are my portion and I hope in you.[3]

Your mercies beseech me to present my body as a living sacrifice, holy and acceptable to you, for this is my reasonable service. Lord, I give you my all, and I know that you are transforming me by the renewing of my mind that I might prove what is that good and acceptable and perfect will of God.[4]

Blessed be God, the Father of my Lord Jesus Christ, the Father of mercies, and the God of all comfort. Thank you for comforting me in all my tribulation, so that I might give comfort to others who are in trouble. Teach me to minister comfort and mercy to others, even as you have ministered to me.[5]

Help me to fulfill your joy by being likeminded with you, in fellowship with your Spirit, full of mercy. Let your mind be in me, Lord.[6] In faith and obedience, I put on an attitude of mercy, kindness, humbleness of mind and longsuffering. And above all else, I put on love which is the bond of perfectness.[7]

Lord, you are my Shepherd. I shall not want. Surely goodness and mercy shall follow me all the days of my life: and I will dwell in the house of the Lord forever.[8]

References: (1)*Psalms 103:4,8* (2)*Psalms 63:3*
(3)*Lamentations 3:22-24* (4)*Romans 12:1* (5)*2 Corinthians 1:3,4*
(6)*Philippians 2:1-5* (7)*Colossians 3:12-14* (8)*Psalms 23*
Other Scriptures: Psalms 108:4, Matthew 5:7, Matthew 9:13, Titus 3:5

78
Walking in Unity

Key Thought: Bridge-building unites those who are separated.

Key Scripture: *"That they all may be one; as thou, Father, art in me, and I in thee, that they also may be one in us: that the world may believe that thou hast sent me" (John 17:21).*

Prayer: Thank you, Lord Jesus, for praying for us. I want your desire for unity in your body to become my desire as well. Enable me do all within my ability to help usher in the unity for which you prayed.

You have asked the Father that we be made perfect in you. It is this unity that will make the world know that the Father sent you, and that He loves each person as He loves you.[1]

Reunite your body, Lord, for it is good and pleasant for brethren to dwell together in unity. It is like the precious ointment upon the head and the dew of Hermon. It is as the dew that descended upon the mountains of Zion, for there you have commanded the blessing, even life forevermore.[2]

Give me grace in every situation to work toward unity, Lord. With all lowliness and meekness, with longsuffering, I want to learn how to forbear with others in love, endeavoring to keep the unity of the Spirit in the bond of peace.[3]

Thank you for setting this goal for us: Till we all come in the unity of the faith, and of the knowledge of the Son of God, unto a perfect man, unto the measure of the stature of the fullness of Christ.[4]

Because we have one Father and one Spirit, Lord, there should never be division among your people.[3] There is one fold and one Shepherd. Lord Jesus, you are the Good Shepherd of the sheep. Thank you for knowing me and protecting me;[5] help me always to know your voice and follow your leading.[6]

It is my earnest desire to be one with you as you are one with your Father, Lord.[1] Help your church to fulfill your joy by becoming likeminded, having the same love, being of one accord, of one mind.[7] Help us all to remember that the Holy Spirit came to your Church when the people were in one accord.[8] Pour forth your abundant graces of love, harmony and unity in my life and relationships and in your Church. Amen.

References: (1)John 17 (2)Psalms 133:1-3 (3)Ephesians 4:2-6 (4)Ephesians 4:13 (5)John 10:14-16 (6)John 10:4-5 (7)Philippians 2:2 (8)Acts 2:1 **Other Scriptures:** *John 10:30, Philippians 1:27*

PRAYERS FOR OTHERS

79

Another's Employment

Key Thought: God is working His purposes out.

Key Scripture: *"And that ye study to be quiet, and to do your own business, and to work with your own hands, as we commanded you: That ye may walk honestly toward them that are without, and that ye may have lack of nothing" (1 Thess. 4:11, 12).*

Prayer: Lord, I am certain that it is not your will for _____ to be out of work. Make a way for him/her so that he/she will once again feel productive and will not have to owe anything to any man except to love him.[1]

Strengthen _____ to do the work you have called him/her to do. Let not his/her hands be weak. Help him/her know that you do have a special job for him/her to do and his/her work will be rewarded.[2]

Help _____ to count it all joy when things don't work out as he/she hopes, realizing that the trying of his/her faith works patience into his/her life. Let patience have its perfect work in _____ 's life so that he/she may be perfect and entire, wanting nothing.[3]

Let _____ believe on you even when he/she is not working. Help him/her to see that his/her faith is counted as righteousness,[4] and that all good things stem from faith in you. You are the Giver of every good and perfect gift, the Father of lights, with whom there is no variableness nor shadow of turning.[5] Praise you, Father!

Father, your Word says that where there is no vision the people perish.[6] If _____ lacks a vision of his/her eternal purpose, give vision; if his/her vision has diminished or been lost, restore it.

You, Lord, have the power to put down the mighty from their seats, and the power to exalt those of low degree.[7] Make a place of employment for _____ that will utilize all the special gifts and talents you have given to him/her.

Help _____ to trust in you with all his/her heart and to lean not to his/her own understanding, but to acknowledge you in all his/her ways, knowing that you will direct his/her paths.[8] Give grace to _____ so that he/she will be able to say with Paul, "I know how to be abased, and I know how to abound: every where and in all things I am instructed both to be full and to be hungry, both to abound and to suffer need."[9] Remind him/her that he/she can do all things through Christ which strengthens him/her.[10]

References: *(1)Romans 13:8 (2)2 Chronicles 15:7 (3)James 1:1-4 (4)Galatians 3:6 (5)James 1:17 (6)Proverbs 29:18 (7)Luke 1:52 (8)Proverbs 3:5,6 (9)Philippians 4:12 (10)Philippians 4:13*
Other Scriptures: *Proverbs 4:7,8, Proverbs 21:5, Jeremiah 1:12*

80

Financial Needs of Another

Key Thought: Riches, wealth and honor come from God.

Key Scripture: *"Beloved, I wish above all things that thou mayest prosper and be in health, even as thy soul prospereth" (3 John 2).*

Prayer: Heavenly Father, I come to you now in behalf of _____ who is/are experiencing financial hardship. Your Word declares that you want your people to prosper. I come against anything that may exist in _____'s life/lives that prevents him/her/them from receiving the blessing of prosperity which you have promised to your children, in the name of Jesus Christ, my Lord.

Lord, make his/her/their way prosperous.[1] Send prosperity now.[2] Your Word declares, "The God of heaven will prosper us,"[3] and I beseech you, Father, to bring prosperity to _____. Remind _____ _____ of his/her/their need to seek you in the same way that Uzziah sought you, for you have shown that as long as Uzziah sought you, you made him to prosper.[4] Help _____ to seek you and your righteousness first, realizing that if he/she/they do(es) so, you will add all that he/she/they need(s) to his/her/their life/lives.[5]

May _____ never forsake you, Lord. You cannot prosper those who forsake you.[6] Give him/her/them courage and strength; keep him/her/them from all discouragement.[7] Empower him/her/them to fulfill your statutes so that you can prosper him/her/them.[8] As he/she/they learn(s) to walk in your ways, Lord, you will prosper him/her/them.

Be with _____ in this time of need, a very present help to him/her/them. Make all that he/she/they do(es) to prosper.[9] Wealth and riches are a gift from your hands, Father, and I pray that you will bestow your blessings upon _____.

Give him/her/them the faith to appropriate your promises,
Lord. Blessed is the person who fears you and delights in
your commandments; wealth and riches shall be in
his/her/their house.[10] Praise you, Father. Unleash your
power, Lord, and bless _____
with financial prosperity.

References: *(1)Isaiah 48:15 (2)Psalms 118:25 (3)Nehemiah 2:20*
(4)2 Chronicles 26:5 (5)Matthew 6:33 (6)2 Chronicles 24:20
(7)1 Chronicles 22:13 (8)1 Kings 2:3 (9)Genesis 39:3
(10)Psalms 112:3 ***Other Scriptures:*** *Deuteronomy 8:18,*
Ecclesiastes 5:19, Ecclesiastes 7:12, Ecclesiastes 10:19

81
Another's Healing

Key Thought: God heals. Jesus was the expression of
God's willingness to heal.

Key Scripture: *"And Jesus went about all Galilee, teaching
in their synagogues, and preaching the gospel of the
kingdom, and healing all manner of sickness and all
manner of disease among the people"* (Matthew 4:23).

Prayer: Heavenly Father, thank you for your healing power
and for your desire to heal your people. I come to you now
on behalf of _____ who suffers from
_____. I ask you, Lord, to heal his/her body
and to restore him/her to complete health in you.

There is a balm in Gilead,[1] Lord, and you are the One
who brings healing to the human body. You created our
bodies and you are the Great Physician who knows exactly
what we need in order to be well. Lord Jesus, you
commanded your disciples to heal the sick[2] and you healed
all who were brought to you.[3] Your Word says that with
your stripes we are healed[4] and that you are the Lord who

heals us.[5] You, Lord, took our infirmities and carried our diseases.[6] You are the same yesterday, today and forever.[7] You said to pray for one another that we may be healed.[8] And, that the prayer of faith will save the sick and you will raise him up.[9] In faith, I now bring _____ _____ to you, and I beseech you, Lord, to heal him/her even as you healed the lame, blind and afflicted when you walked the earth.[10] All power in heaven and earth is yours, O Lord;[11] impart your supernatural healing power to _____ _____.

Send healing on the wings of your Spirit, Lord,[12] to him/her. You have promised to be his/her healer. Do not permit this affliction to remain with him/her.

Bless the Lord, O my soul. All that is within me bless your holy name. I will not forget your benefits, Lord. You forgive all our iniquities and you heal all our diseases.[13]

I hope in you, O Lord. I will ever praise you.[14] Thank you for being health to _____ and for healing him/her. Glory be to your name forever and ever.

References: (1)Jeremiah 8:22 (2)Matthew 10:8 (3)Matthew 9:35 (4)Isaiah 53:5 (5)Exodus 15:26 (6)Matthew 8:17 (7)Hebrews 13:8 (8)James 5:16 (9)James 5:15 (10)Luke 4:40 (11)Matthew 28:18 (12)Malachi 4:2 (13)Psalms 103:3 (14)Psalms 42:11
Other Scriptures: Psalms 107:20, Isaiah 58:8, Jeremiah 30:17, Mark 16:18, 1 Corinthians 12:28, James 5:14, 1 Peter 2:24

82

Victims of Infidelity in Marriage

Key Thought: God wants faithfulness in marriage.

Key Scripture: *"Therefore shall a man leave his father and his mother, and shall cleave unto his wife: and they shall be one flesh"* (Gen. 2:24).

Prayer: Heavenly Father, thank you for the sanctity of Christian marriage. I pray for _____ and _____ during this time of crisis in their marriage, asking you to remind them of their wedding vows, their commitment to you and each other.

Remind _____ of his/her need to repent of adultery.[1] Grant repentance to his/her heart. It is your command that we should not commit adultery;[2] help _____ to obey you in this important matter.

For _____, who is the victim of his/her spouse 's adultery, I pray that you will keep him/her from any sense of rejection and bitterness. Help him/her to understand and forgive his/her spouse. Pour out upon him/her a sense of your unconditional love, so that it may flow through him/her to his/her marriage partner.

Bring restoration to this marriage, Lord. Deal tenderly with the adulterous partner as you did with the woman taken in adultery. Speak to his/her heart: "Neither do I condemn thee: go, and sin no more."[3]

Lord, give _____ and _____ a new sense of commitment to their marriage. Help them to submit themselves to each other in fear of you.[4] Help _____ to see the seriousness of his/her sin of adultery and the effects it is having on his/her marriage and family.[5]

I come against Satan who is blinding and deceiving _____, and trying to destroy this precious family.[6] Satan, in the name of Jesus and on the authority of God's Word,[7] I command you to stop your mission of destruction against this family, now!

Thank you, Father, for undertaking in behalf of _____ and _____. Help them and bless them.

References: (1)*James 2:11* (2)*Mark 10:19* (3)*John 8:3-11* (4)*Ephesians 5:21* (5)*Luke 18:20* (6)*John 10:10* (7)*Luke 10:18,19* **Other Scriptures:** *Exodus 20:14, Proverbs 5:15-19, Jeremiah 1:12, Galatians 5:19*

83

Ministry of Intercession

Key Thought: He prays best who loves best.

Key Scripture: *"And I sought for a man among them, that should make up the hedge, and stand in the gap before me for the land, that I should not destroy it: but I found none"* *(Ezek. 22:30).*

Prayer: Thank you, Father, for Jesus, who ever lives to make intercession for us.[1] You have poured forth your Spirit of grace and supplication upon me.[2] He helps me when I don't know how to pray as I should. Thank you for your Spirit who makes intercession for us with groanings which cannot be uttered. You search our hearts and know what the mind of the Spirit is, and you make intercession for us according to your will.[3]

Lord, teach me to be an intercessor. I want to be able to stand in the gap before you.[4] I want to lift up others to you in prayer, faithfully interceding for them in your presence.

You are looking for intercessors.[5] I respond to your call, Lord. I will call upon you continually; I will stir myself up to take hold of you.[6] Thank you for your gift of righteousness, Lord, for I know that the effectual, fervent prayer of a righteous man avails much.[7] Thank you for the blessings of intercessory prayer.

When I pray, Lord, give me much grace and increase my faith level, so that I will believe I have received what I have prayed.[8] You have promised to give me the things I desire when I learn to pray effectually, in faith, without wavering.[9]

You have posted me as a watchman on your walls. I will never be silent day or night. I will call on you, Lord, I will give myself no rest and I will give you no rest until you establish Jerusalem as a praise in the earth.[10] Until your plans and purposes are fulfilled and your glory covers the earth, Lord, as the waters cover the sea,[11] I will pray and travail, Lord, until Christ is fully formed in me.[12] Let your kingdom come, Lord.[13]

With all prayer and supplication in the Spirit, and watching thereunto with all perseverance and supplication for all the saints, I now pray in the Holy Spirit[14] with full assurance that you are already undertaking in behalf of my prayers.

I pray specifically now for _____.
Lord, meet each need of the people for whom I pray. I ask you to accomplish the following specific things in their lives: _____.

I pray in your name, Lord, in the name of Jesus. I pray according to your will as revealed in your Word. As a result of this, I know that my prayers will avail much. The result is wonderful joy, peace, and confidence. Thank you, Lord.

References: (1)Hebrews 7:25 (2)Zechariah 12:10 (3)Romans 8:26-27 (4)Ezekiel 22:30 (5)Isaiah 59:16 (6)Isaiah 64:7 (7)James 5:16 (8)Mark 11:24 (9)James 1:6 (10)Isaiah 62:6,7

(11)Habakkuk 2:14 (12)Galatians 4:19 (13)Matthew 6:10
*(14)Ephesians 6:18 **Other Scriptures:** John 16:23,24,26*

84

Someone Who Has Lost a Loved One

Key Thought: The God of all comfort uses us to comfort others.

Key Scripture: *"Yea, though I walk through the valley of the shadow of death, I will fear no evil: for thou art with me: thy rod and thy staff they comfort me" (Ps. 23:4).*

Prayer: Heavenly Father, I pray for _____ who has lost his/her _____. Be very close to him/her during this time of grief and mourning.

Assure him/her that those who mourn will be comforted.[1] Your Holy Spirit is the Comforter, and He has the power to turn his/her mourning into dancing.[2] Lord, give him/her this kind of assurance and the peace that passeth all understanding.[3]

Help me to be a source of comfort to him/her during this difficult time. Blessed be your name, Father. You are the Father of our Lord Jesus Christ, the Father of mercies and the God of all comfort.[4] Bring comfort to _____ _____ through your Holy Spirit.

To every thing there is a season, as your Word points out: a time to be born and a time to die, a time to weep, and a time to laugh, a time to mourn and a time to dance.[5] Help _____ to see that you are working your purposes out in his/her life.

Impart hope to _____ during his/her time of sorrow. Let his/her mourning be turned into joy as he/she realizes all that you have provided for him/her and his/her loved ones, to the end that his/her glory will sing praise to you and not be silent.[6] O Lord my God, I give you thanks forever for all that you are doing.

If the loved one _____ has lost was saved, help him/her find consolation in your counsel that we are not to sorrow as those who have no hope[7] for the loved one is safe with you and _____ _____ can rejoice in the anticipation of being reunited with his/her loved one in your presence. There is great comfort in knowing that you, Lord, will one day descend from heaven with a shout with the voice of the archangel, and with the trump of God. The dead in Christ will rise first; then we who are alive and remain shall be caught up together with them in the clouds to meet you in the air. And so shall we ever be with you. Help me with these words to comfort _____ _____ and all who have lost loved ones or who may fear death themselves.

Lord Jesus, help _____ to see your power and to experience your love. Give him/her everlasting consolation and good hope through grace. May these blessings enable him/her to comfort his/her own heart and may they establish him/her in every good word and work.[8]

References: (1)Matthew 5:4 (2)Psalms 30:11 (3)Philippians 4:7 (4)2 Corinthians 1:3,4 (5)Ecclesiastes 3:4 (6)Psalms 30:12 (7)1 Thessalonians 4:13-18 (8)2 Thessalonians 2:16,17

85

Another's Marriage

Key Thought: In Jesus' relationship with the Church we see God's plan for marriage.

Key Scripture: *"For this cause shall a man leave his father and mother, and shall be joined unto his wife, and they two shall be one flesh" (Ephesians 5:31).*

Prayer: Heavenly Father, I come to you now in behalf of _____ and _____. Bless their marriage, Lord, and bring them ever closer to you and each other. When problems arise in their relationship, impart wisdom and love to their hearts so that all problems will be resolved early, in the best possible manner.

I thank you for this couple, Lord. I know you have many plans and purposes for them. Help _____ _____ to love his wife as you, Lord Jesus, love your Church.[1] Help _____ to submit to her husband as unto you, Lord.[2] Keep them both from the evil one.[3]

Help them, Father, to preserve their unity as husband and wife in the Spirit. Keep them from all bitterness;[4] may sweetness always be the characteristic of their marriage. May others be drawn to your love when they see _____ _____ and _____ living for you and for each other in the blessings of Christian love.

Thank you for the gift of marriage, Father. It is honorable in all. Show _____ and _____ _____ that they honor you through their marriage and teach them that the marriage bed is undefiled, enabling them to fulfill your will that they become one flesh.[5]

May _____ be drawn ever closer to you when he beholds _____'s life adorned by a meek and quiet spirit which is of great price in your sight, Father.[6] Help her to be sober, to love her husband, to be discreet, chaste, a good housekeeper, and obedient to her husband.[7] Help _____ to love his wife for this is well pleasing to you, Lord. Enable him to teach his wife through his example, to wash her with the water of your Word,[8] to protect her and to keep her only unto himself throughout the years.

Father, preserve this marriage. Remind _____ _____ and _____ of their vows to each other and to you. Remind them of their need to pray together daily. Bless them in every way.

References: (1)*Ephesians 5:24,25* (2)*Ephesians 5:22* (3)*John 17:15* (4)*Colossians 3:18,19* (5)*Hebrews 13:4* (6)*1 Peter 3:4* (7)*Titus 2:4,5* (8)*Ephesians 5:26* **Other Scriptures:** *Esther 1:20, 1 Corinthians 7:10, 1 Corinthians 7:33, 1 Corinthians 7:34*

86

Single Believer Desiring Marriage

Key Thought: God ordained marriage for His divine blessing.

Key Scripture: *"Therefore shall a man leave his father and mother, and shall cleave unto his wife: and they shall be one flesh" (Gen. 2:24).*

Prayer: Thank you, Father, for instituting marriage to bless your children. I come now to pray for _____ who desires to be married. I ask that you guide him/her clearly in the choice of the person you have prepared as his/her mate.

Let him/her trust in you with all his/her heart, and not lean to his/her own understanding. May he/she acknowledge you in all his/her ways as you direct his/her path.[1]

I pray for him/her that he/she will readily incline his/her ear unto your wisdom and understanding as you speak to his/her heart.[2] You, Lord, are his/her confidence, and will keep his/her foot trom being taken.[3]

May he/she and his/her future husband/wife be wise in understanding what your will is,[4] and in righteousness and holiness submit themselves one to the other in the reverent fear of God.[5]

I pray that in their marriage the wife will submit herself to her husband as unto the Lord.[6] And that the husband will love his wife even as Christ loved the Church and gave himself for it.[7]

Father, let your favor be great toward them,[8] and let them fulfil your joy by being followers of God, as dear children, walking in love as Christ also has loved them.[9]

References: (1)*Proverbs 3:5,6* (2)*Proverbs 2:2* (3)*Proverbs 3:26*
(4)*Ephesians 5:17* (5)*Ephesians 5:21* (6)*Ephesians 5:22*
(7)*Ephesians 5:26* (8)*Proverbs 19:22* (9)*Ephesians 5:2.*

87

A Nation and Its Leaders

Key Thought: Blessed is the nation whose god is the Lord.

Key Scripture: *"I exhort therefore, that supplications, prayers, intercessions, and giving of thanks, be made for all men; for kings, and for all that are in authority; that we may lead a quiet and peaceable life in all godliness and honesty"* (1 Tim. 2:1,2).

Prayer: Father, thank you for our leaders. I pray for all those in authority in this nation. Those in government, in school systems, in the legal system, in churches, in the media, and all other positions of influence. That your people may live quiet and peaceable lives in all godliness and honesty. For this is good and acceptable in your sight.[1]

You have said that when the righteous are in authority, the people rejoice: but when the wicked rule, the people mourn.² Establish your justice and make the wrong things right in our nation and our leadership.³

Give us righteous leadership, Lord. Open a door of the gospel to any leaders who are not saved and born again.⁴ Let your Word come to them and pierce their hearts.⁵ Let it be like fire and like a hammer that breaks the rock into pieces.⁶ Let them joyfully receive Jesus as Lord and become children of God.⁷

Father, the king's heart and the heart of every leader is in your hand. You turn them wherever you will.⁸ Turn all of our leaders' hearts in the way of your wisdom. Let their actions and words be in agreement with your plans and purposes.

I pray, Lord, that your people, throughout this whole nation, who are called by your name, will humble themselves, and pray, and seek your face, and turn from their wicked ways. Then you will hear from heaven, and will forgive their sin, and heal their land.⁹ Do it, Lord. Heal our land. Pour your mercy and grace upon us. Let your kingdom come and your will be done in this nation, and in all the earth, as it is in heaven.¹⁰

References: (1)1 Timothy 2:2,3 (2)Proverbs 29:2 (3)Luke 11:13 (4)Colossians 4:3 (5)Hebrews 4:12 (6)Jeremiah 23:29 (7)1 John 3:1 (8)Proverbs 21:1 (9)2 Chronicles 7:14. (10)Matthew 6:10.

88

To Know the Reality of the New Birth

Key Thought: We have been born anew of the Spirit of God.

Key Scripture: *"These things have I written unto you that believe on the name of the Son of God; that ye may know that ye have eternal life, and that ye may believe on the name of the Son of God" (1 John 5:13).*

Prayer: Heavenly Father, thank you for giving us eternal life through your Son. I lift up _____ to you now because he/she is having a difficult time believing the promises of your Word that he/she has been born again. The devil would like nothing more than to confuse _____ by bringing doubts to his/her mind concerning your free gift of salvation. Rebuke the enemy, Lord, in behalf of _____, and grant him/her a complete assurance of your salvation and your love for him/her.

Remind _____ of the truth that he/she has been buried with you into death. As you rose from the dead, Lord Jesus, so has _____ risen to walk in newness of life with you.[1] Restore unto him/her the joy of your salvation[2] and the sense of wonder and newness that you give to your children.

Help _____ serve you in newness of spirit.[3] Let your Spirit so work in his/her heart and life that he/she will be reminded of all you have done for him/her. _____'s life is in you, Lord Jesus, and, therefore, he/she is a new creature.[4] The old things are passed away; behold, all things have become new in _____'s life.[5] Thank you, Father, for the newness of life you give to your children.

Renew _____ in the spirit of his/her mind. Help him/her to lay aside all doubts concerning your transforming power in his/her life. Help him/her to put on the new man, which after God is created in righteousness and true holiness.[6] Remind _____ of the truth that whosoever believes in

Jesus as the Christ is born of you.[7] Help him/her to remember that whosoever is born of God is able to overcome the world through faith.[8] Remind him/her that he/she has the power to place the helmet of salvation firmly on his/her head, and that he/she must take the shield of faith to quench the fiery darts of the enemy.[9] Thank you, Father, that you are at work in _____'s life.

References: (1)Romans 6:4 (2)Psalms 51:12 (3)Romans 7:6 (4)Galatians 6:15 (5)2 Corinthians 5:17 (6)Ephesians 4:24 (7)1 John 4:15 (8)1 John 5:4 (9)Ephesians 6:16,17
Other Scriptures: 1 John 3:1, 1 John 3:21, 1 John 4:2

89
Freedom From the Occult

Key Thought: Jesus came to set the captives free.

Key Scripture: *"For I am persuaded, that neither death, nor life, nor angels, nor principalities, nor powers, nor things present, nor things to come, nor height, nor depth, nor any other creature, shall be able to separate us from the love of God, which is in Christ Jesus our Lord"* (Rom. 8:38-39).

Prayer: Father, I come to you on behalf of _____ _____ who is involved in the occult practice of _____.

I thank you that your Word that goes out of your mouth will not return to you void, but it shall accomplish that which you please and it shall prosper in the thing for which you send it.[1]

Jesus, you came to destroy the works of the devil.[2] And in your death, burial and resurrection you disarmed principalities and powers, and made a spectacle of them, truimphing over them.[3]

Lord, you said if we ask anything in your name you will do it.[4] I know you delight in setting people free from the bondage of occultism, and taking back the spoils of the enemy.[5]

Therefore, Father, I ask you in the name of Jesus, and by His blood, to send your Holy Spirit into _____ _____'s life, and set him/her free from the control and deception of this occult practice. Let your Spirit convince him/her of sin and righteousness and judgement,[6] and guide him/her into the truth.[7]

Send people to minister to him/her, to open his/her eyes, and to turn him/her from darkness to light and from the power of Satan unto the power of God.[8] Send your ministering angels to do battle, on behalf of him/her, against the forces of darkness.[9]

Father, I ask that _____ be totally loosed and set free from all occultism, receive Jesus as his/her Lord, and be delivered from the power of darkness and translated into the kingdom of Jesus, the Son of your love.[10]

References: *(1)Isaiah 55:11 (2)1 John 3:8 (3)Colossians 2:15 (4)John 14:14 (5)Matthew 12:29(6)John 16:8 (7)John 16:13 (8)Acts 26:16-18 (9)Hebrews 1:14 (10)Colossians 1:13.*

90

A Hedge of Protection

Key Thought: The shield of faith quenches all the fiery darts of the wicked one.

Key Scripture: *"Hast not thou made an hedge about him, and about his house, and about all that he hath on every side? Thou hast blessed the work of his hands, and his substance is increased in the land" (Job 1:10).*

Prayer: Lord God Almighty, I commit _____ into your care and safekeeping. May your ministering angels watch over him/her.[1] I place his/her hand in yours with the confidence that comes from knowing that you will take good care of your property.

You said, Lord, that you would be a wall of fire round about him/her, and that you will be the glory in the midst of him/her. Praise your name.[2]

The angel of the Lord encamps around all those who fear you, and you deliver them.[3] Assign a guardian angel to _____, Lord, so that no evil will befall him/her. Protect him/her from the evil one.

I lift up _____ to you and I ask you to watch over him/her like a mother hen watches over her chicks[4] and a shepherd watches over his sheep.[5] Teach _____ that he who dwells in the secret place of the most High shall abide under the shadow of the Almighty.[6] You are his/her fortress.[7] May he/she learn to trust in you implicitly.

Cover him/her with your feathers so that under your wings he/she will safely trust.[8] Let your truth become his/her shield and buckler so that he/she will not be afraid for the terror by night nor for the destruction that wastes at noonday.[9]

Bless _____ with a knowledge of your presence, Lord. Let _____ know that when he/she calls upon you, you will answer him/her. You will be with him/her in trouble. You will deliver him/her and honor him/her. Satisfy him/her with long life and show him/her your salvation.[10]

References: (1)*Hebrews 1:13,14* (2)*Zechariah 2:5* (3)*Psalms 34:7*
(4)*Matthew 23:37* (5)*John 10:11* (6)*Psalms 91:1* (7)*Psalms 18:2*
(8)*Psalms 17:8* (9)*Psalms 91:4-6* (10)*Psalms 91:15,16*
Other Scriptures: Luke 10:5,6, Luke 21:18, Hebrews 13:6

91

To Be Restored to Fellowship

Key Thought: Nothing will separate us from the love of God.

Key Scripture: *"Brethren, if a man be overtaken in a fault, ye which are spiritual, restore such an one in the spirit of meekness; considering thyself, lest thou also be tempted. Bear ye one another's burdens, and so fulfill the law of Christ"* (Gal. 6:1, 2).

Prayer: Heavenly Father, I thank you for giving me a ministry of reconciliation to _____. Help me to minister to him/her in the power of your Spirit.

All things are of you, Father. You have reconciled me to yourself by Jesus Christ, and you have given me the ministry of reconciliation. In Christ you are reconciling the world unto yourself. You made Him who knew no sin to become sin for us.[1] Bring reconciliation, Lord, to _____ who once walked with you.

We who are strong ought to bear the infirmities of the weak, and not to please ourselves.[2] Teach me to bear the infirmities of _____ through love and prayer. May he/she be brought back to you, Lord.

Remind _____ that you are the Bread of Life,[3] Lord, and that to find true satisfaction in this life he/she needs to return to you. Establish him/her in the faith and make him/her ever mindful of his/her need to continue in the things which he/she learned and of which he/she was assured.[4]

Thank you for the promises of your Word, Father, which in Jesus are all yea and amen.[5] You see all our ways, and I thank you that you have taken notice of the ways of _____ as well. Your promise is that you will heal him/her and restore your comforts unto him/her.[6] Thank you, Lord.

Your sheep hear your voice and you know them, Lord. You give your sheep eternal life and they shall never perish. No man shall be able to pluck your sheep from your hands.[7] He who comes to you, you will in no wise cast out.[8] Thank you, Lord, for being willing to leave the ninety-nine sheep in your fold and go out to find the one that is lost.[9] I rejoice in you because I know you will find _____ and bring him/her back into your fold. He/she will hear your voice and respond. Speak to him/her, Lord.

*References: (1)2 Corinthians 5:18-21 (2)Romans 15:1 (3)John 6:48 (4)2 Timothy 3:14 (5)2 Corinthians 1:20 (6)Isaiah 57:18 (7)John 10:28,29 (8)John 6:37 (9)Luke 15:4 **Other Scriptures:** Ephesians 1:17*

92

Salvation of Another

Key Thought: God is not willing that any should perish.

Key Scripture: *"Wherefore he is able also to save them to the uttermost that come unto God by him, seeing he ever liveth to make intercession for them" (Heb. 7:25).*

Prayer: Heavenly Father, I thank you for the gift of salvation that is received through faith in your Son, my

Lord Jesus Christ. Thank you that you are not willing that any should perish, but that all should come to repentance.[1]

I come to you now on behalf of _____ who needs Jesus as his/her Savior and Lord.

I pray that _____ be delivered from every scheme and snare that the devil has used to hold him/her captive.[2] Let every stronghold of unbelief and vain imagination in _____'s life be pulled down and brought into captivity to the obedience of Christ.[3]

Work in _____'s life so that he/she will realize that he/she must call upon you in order to be saved.[4] I ask you as Lord of the harvest to send laborers to share the gospel with _____.[5] Let them minister your Word, Lord, in the power of your Spirit to make _____ wise unto salvation through faith in Christ Jesus,[6] to open his/her eyes, and to turn him/her from darkness to light and from the power of Satan to the power of God, that he/she may receive forgiveness of sins, and inheritance among those who are sanctified and set apart by faith in you.[7]

Thank you, Lord, that you are working and active in _____'s life, calling him/her into your love and salvation.

References: (1)*2 Peter 3:9* (2)*2 Timothy 2:26* (3)*2 Corinthians 10:4,5* (4)*Romans 10:13* (5)*Luke 10:2* (6)*2 Timothy 3:15* (7)*Acts 26:18* **Other Scriptures:** *Acts 2:21, Romans 1:16, 1 Thessalonians 5:9, 1 Timothy 2:1-6, 2 Timothy 1:9, 2 Timothy 2:10*

93

Salvation of a Loved One

Key Thought: God will draw your loved one to himself in response to your prayer.

Key Scripture: *"The Lord is not slack concerning his promise, as some men count slackness; but is longsuffering to usward, not willing that any should perish, but that all should come to repentance" (2 Pet. 3:9).*

Prayer: Heavenly Father, by the wooing of the Holy Spirit, draw _____ to yourself. Help him/her to see that Jesus Christ is real and that He has the power to save to the uttermost all who come to God by Him. Thank you, Lord Jesus, for making intercession with me for _____ _____.[1]

Help _____ to see his/her need for repentance. You are near, Lord, to all who have a broken heart, and you save those who be of a contrite spirit.[2] Bring brokenness to _____ so he/she will see his/her need for you.

Thank you for your promise, Father, that whosoever will call upon your name shall be saved.[3] So work in the life of _____ that he/she will call upon your name.[4]

Be very close to _____. May he/she sense your presence and understand that your grace is at work in his/her life. Show him/her that he/she does not have to be perfect in order to be accepted by you, but all he/she has to do is to trust in you.[5] By your grace, through faith, he/she will be saved,[6] and he/she will know that such a gift does not come through works of righteousness but simply through your gracious love.[7]

Help _____ to see that unless he/she repents and accepts you as his/her Savior and Lord, he/she will perish.[8] It is not your will for him/her to perish.[9] Help me, Father, to be a good witness to him/her and to pray for him/her often. If it be your will, use me to convert

_____ from the error of his/her way, and in so doing, I know I will save his/her soul from death.[10]

Send just the right persons to _____ to share the gospel of Jesus Christ with him/her. And let them speak your words to him/her that he/she may accept Jesus as his/her Lord and Savior and become your child.[11]

Thank you for sending your Son, Father, that whosoever would believe in Jesus should not perish, but have everlasting life.[12] I express faith to you now for the salvation of _____. Thank you for giving him/her eternal life.

References: *(1)Hebrews 7:25 (2)Psalms 34:18 (3)Acts 2:21 (4)Romans 10:13 (5)Romans 3:22,23 (6)Ephesians 2:8,9 (7)Titus 3:5 (8)Luke 13:3 (9)2 Peter 3:9 (10)James 5:20 (11)John 1:12 (12)John 3:16* **Other Scriptures:** *1 Corinthians 9:22, 2 Thessalonians 2:10*

94

Someone Undergoing a Satanic Attack

Key Thought: Satan is a defeated foe.

Key Scripture: *"No weapon that is formed against thee shall prosper; and every tongue that shall rise against thee in judgment thou shalt condemn. This is the heritage of the servants of the Lord, and their righteousness is of me, saith the Lord" (Isaiah 54:17).*

Prayer: Heavenly Father, I thank you for the promises of your Word. I claim your promises now in behalf of _____ who is undergoing an attack from the enemy in the area of _____ in his/her life. I thank you that the gates of hell cannot prevail against your people, the Church.[1] I thank you for the equipment and weapons you have given to us to fight against the enemy. I thank you for the armor of God and for the sword of the Spirit which is the Word of God.[2]

Lord, you said in your Word that you have given your children authority over all the power of the enemy and nothing shall by any means hurt us.[3] You also said if we would submit to you and resist the devil, he would flee from us.[4]

Therefore, I resist you, Satan, in the name of Jesus and I command you to stop interfering in _____ _____'s life. You have no right to touch him/her for he/she is a child of the King.

Thank you, Lord, that you do not have to save us with sword and spear.[5] The weapons of our warfare are not carnal, but they are mighty to the tearing down of satanic strongholds.[6] Help _____ to remember who you are, that you are fighting for him/her, that all power in heaven and earth are yours, and that you will deliver him/her from the influence of the enemy.[7] Help him/her to remember that the battle really is yours, not his/hers, and that if he/she will stand on your Word, in your name, by the power of the Holy Spirit, Satan will flee from him/her.[8]

Reveal to _____ his/her need to call upon you in the day of trouble, for you will deliver him/her, and then he/she will be able to glorify you.[9] Be pleased, O Lord, to deliver him/her; make haste to help him/her. Let his/her supplication come before you; deliver him/her according to your Word.[10]

Lord, you are _____'s defense.[11] You are the Rock of his/her refuge.[12] Help him/her find shelter in the blessed promises and provisions of your Word, Father. Let _____ wage a good warfare, Lord, holding onto his/her faith, and a good conscience.[13]

Thank you that no enemy can defeat us; I praise you, Father,
that nothing will be able to separate _____
from your love.[14]

References: (1)*Matthew 16:18* (2)*Ephesians 6:13,17* (3)*Luke 10:19*
(4)*James 4:7* (5)*1 Samuel 17:47* (6)*2 Corinthians 10:4*
(7)*Psalms 40:13* (8)*2 Chronicles 20:15* (9)*Psalms 50:15*
(10)*Psalms 119:170* (11)*Psalms 89:18* (12)*Psalms 94:22*
(13)*1 Timothy 1:18,19* (14)*Romans 8:39*

95
A Single Believer

Key Thought: The single person does not have to be lonely.

Key Scripture: *"Turn,…saith the Lord; for I am married
unto you…and I will bring you to Zion: and I will give you
pastors according to mine heart, which shall feed you with
knowledge and understanding" (Jer. 3:14,15).*

Prayer: Heavenly Father, I come to you now in behalf of
_____ who is single. Keep him/her from all
loneliness, immorality and discouragement. Lord, you have
promised to be with us in whatsoever state we find ourselves
and I pray that you will bless _____.

Provide all his/her needs as he/she waits on you.
Reveal your will regarding marriage to him/her and help
him/her to await your perfect timing in all things without
growing impatient. Help him/her to be content as a single
person serving you[1] unless and until you show him/her to
marry.

Help him/her to flee fornication for certainly the
pressures upon single people in the realm of sexuality are
great today. Help him/her to remember that you, Lord
Jesus, bought him/her with a price; therefore, it is his/her

responsibility to glorify you in his/her body and spirit which are yours.[2]

Help _____ to flee youthful lusts and to follow righteousness, faith, charity and peace with those who call on you out of a pure heart.[3] Help _____ to know the fulness of your love, Father. Rejoice over him/her as the bridegroom rejoices over his bride.[4] Let him/her respond to you with eagerness and joy, Lord, as you draw him/her to yourself.

Show your Church how to respond to single people with familial love that will help them to feel accepted, a real part of your body, Lord. Surround _____ with the fellowship of believers who know how to minister to him/her. Join _____ unto you in the unity of your Spirit, Lord. May he/she learn to use this period of singleness to draw very close to you, Lord, and to serve you with all his/her heart.

*References: (1)Philippians 4:11 (2)1 Corinthians 6:17-20 (3)2 Timothy 2:22 (4)Isaiah 62:5 **Other Scriptures:** Proverbs 8:8, Proverbs 19:14, Ephesians 5:22,23, Philippians 2:12,15,16*

96

A Student

Key Thought: Wisdom gives life to those who have it.

Key Scripture: *"Study to shew thyself approved unto God, a workman that needeth not to be ashamed, rightly dividing the word of truth" (2 Tim. 2:15).*

Prayer: Father, I pray for _____ who is facing all the challenges and difficulties of school responsibilities. Impart your wisdom to him/her so that he/she will understand that wisdom is the principal thing.[1]

Motivate him/her to seek wisdom and to gain understanding.[2]

You are a very present help to _____ in all areas of his/her life.[3] Help him/her to call upon you when the demands of scholastic life threaten to overwhelm him/her.

May _____ realize that you have a plan and purpose for his/her life.[4] Give him/her the motivation to pursue your goals for him/her. Protect him/her from all harmful influences.

Keep his/her mind stayed on you.[5] When philosophies and theories of this world oppose his/her faith, help him/her to maintain a constant focus on you, to run his/her course with patience, looking unto you, Lord Jesus, the author and finisher of our faith.[6]

May I always be faithful with my responsibilities to _____, to pray for him/her, to look for ways to encourage him/her, to listen to him/her and to provide helpful counsel to him/her. Help me to be a true friend to him/her, one who loves at all times and never gives up.[7]

Bless _____ with clarity of mind as he/she studies. Keep him/her from the error of procrastination concerning assignments. Remind him/her to remain faithful even in the things he or she may consider unimportant.[8]

Thank you for providing us with all we need to meet the challenges of life. You have equipped _____ _____ with the necessary abilities to do well in school. Help _____ to remember to be thankful to you for all you have given to him/her.[9]

Although it is sometimes true that much study is a weariness of the flesh,[10] I pray for _____ that you will renew his/her strength. Help him/her to mount up with wings as an eagle and to run and not be weary in all his/her scholastic endeavors.[11] Strengthen him/her with all might in his/her inner man, that you, Lord Jesus Christ, would dwell in his/her heart by faith and that he/she would be rooted and grounded in your love.[12]

Keep him/her in the center of your will. Prevent him/her from being tossed to and fro, and carried about with every wind of doctrine, by the sleight of men, and cunning craftiness.[13]

I pray for _____, Lord Jesus, that you would enable him/her to grow up in you in all things.[14] Help him/her to learn your ways. Lead him/her in the paths of righteousness.[15] May he/she always remember that the fear (respect, reverence) of the Lord is the beginning of all wisdom.[16]

Bring friends to _____ who will be a source of great encouragement to him/her. Protect him/her from the evil one.[17]

May his/her greatest desire always be to follow in your steps, Lord.[18] Bless him/her and use him/her to bring glory to your name.

References: (1)Proverbs 4:7 (2)Proverbs 4:5 (3)Psalms 46:1 (4)Jeremiah 29:11 (5)Isaiah 26:3 (6)Hebrews 12:2 (7)Proverbs 17:17 (8)Luke 16:10 (9)Ephesians 5:20 (10)Ecclesiastes 12:12 (11)Isaiah 40:31 (12)Ephesians 3:16,17 (13)Ephesians 4:14 (14)Ephesians 4:15 (15)Psalms 23:3 (16)Psalms 9:10 (17)Matthew 6:13 (18)1 Peter 2:21

97

A Troubled Youth

Key Thought: God has a plan and a purpose for each young person's life.

Key Scripture: *"Wherewithal shall a young man cleanse his way? by taking heed thereto according to thy word. With my whole heart have I sought thee: O let me not wander from thy commandments. Thy word have I hid in mine heart, that I might not sin against thee"* (Ps. 119:9-11).

Prayer: Heavenly Father, deal with _____ in a special way during this difficult time in his/her life. Keep and protect him/her from the evil one.[1] Let all strategies and schemes of the enemy against his/her life be cancelled, now in the name of Jesus.

Convict _____ of his/her need for you. Draw him/her to abundant life in you.[2] I thank you that you have a plan and purpose for his/her life.[3]

May _____ be like the Prodigal Son who realized in his heart that he needed to return to his father.[4] May _____ return to his family and to you, Father.

Turn the heart of _____ to his/her parents, and the hearts of his/her parents toward him/her.[5] We are living in difficult times of disobedience and rebellion, but you, Lord, are more powerful than all the influences of Satan. Turn any disobedience in _____ _____'s life to the wisdom of the just. I thank you that you are making ready a people who are prepared for you.[6]

Help _____ to remember you in the days of his/her youth, while the evil days come not nor the years draw nigh.[7] Keep him/her from all potentially harmful influences of his/her peer group.

My Father, you are the guide of our youths.[8] I pray for young people in general, and for _____ in particular, that they would find you early and be set free from the prevailing philosophies and behaviors of our day. Accompany _____ with restlessness till he/she finds his/her rest in you.

References: (1)Matthew 6:13 (2)John 10:10 (3)Jeremiah 29:11
(4)Luke 15:11-32 (5)Malachi 4:5,6 (6)Luke 1:16,17
(7)Ecclesiastes 12:1 (8)Jeremiah 3:4 **Other Scriptures:**
Psalms 25:7, Ecclesiastes 11:9,10, Mark 10:20, 2 Timothy 2:22

PRAYERS THAT PREVAIL

PART IV

Prayers for the Church

98

The Universal Church

Key Thought: People are called out of the world to become the Church.

Key Scripture: *"And I say also unto thee, That thou art Peter, and upon this rock I will build my church: and the gates of hell shall not prevail against it"* *(Matt. 16:18).*

Prayer: Lord Jesus Christ, I thank you for your Church, that army of men and women who are building your kingdom around the world. It is a universal Church and its mission is eternal.

You continue to add to your Church daily such as should be saved.[1] Revival fires blaze in your Church in various parts of the world today. Send revival to your universal Church, Lord, so men and women will see your truth and reality at work in the earth today.

Pour out your Spirit of grace for the revival of your Church, Father. Let your people rise up and be strong. Let them do mighty exploits in the name of Jesus.[2] Stir them up through spiritual renewal.

Rebuild, restore, renew and revive your Church, Father. May a heaven-borne revival touch each heart with your love. Help us to respond to all you are doing in your Church today.

Save us from prayerlessness. Keep us from lukewarmness.[3] Give us the grace to return to our first love.[4] Restore unto us the joy of your salvation.[5]

Thank you, Father, for raising Jesus from the dead and for setting Him at your own right hand in the heavenly places, far above all principality and power and might and dominion, and every name that is named, not only in this world, but in that which is to come. Father, you have put all things under the feet of Jesus and you have given Him to be the head over all things to the Church, which is His body, the fullness of Him that fills all in all.[6] Praise your holy name!

Grant repentance to your people, Lord. Blot out the sins of your people. Prepare us for the times of refreshing that will come from your presence.[7] Lord Jesus, you are the head of the Church; you are the Savior of the body.[8] You loved your Church so much that you gave yourself for it, that you might sanctify and cleanse it with the washing of water by the Word. Thank you, Lord, that you are presenting your Church to yourself as a glorious Church, without spot or wrinkle, so that it will be holy and without blemish.[9] Help me to do my part to purify your Church by being obedient to you.

Thank you for allowing me to be part of your great Church, O Lord. Teach me how to behave in your house, the Church of the living God, the pillar and ground of the truth.[10] Bless your Church, Lord. Help your people to know you as the One who searches the reins and hearts,[11] and to remember that you will render unto each of us according to our works.[12] Help us to have an ear to hear what you are saying to your Church in these last days.[13] Even so, come quickly, Lord.[14]

References: (1)Acts 2:47 (2)Daniel 11:32 (3)Revelation 3:16 (4)Revelation 2:4 (5)Psalms 51:12 (6)Ephesians 1:20-23

(7)*Acts 3:19* (8)*Ephesians 5:23* (9)*Ephesians 5:24,27*
(10)*1 Timothy 3:15* (11)*Jeremiah 17:10* (12)*Proverbs 24:12*
(13)*Revelation 3:7* (14)*Revelation 22:20* **Other Scriptures:**
Matthew 16:18, 1 Corinthians 11:18, John 13:35, Colossians 1:24,
Hebrews 13:1, 1 Peter 1:22

99
The Local Church

Key Thought: The local church is a school of God's Spirit.

Key Scripture: *"But now hath God set the members every one of them in the body, as it hath pleased him. And if they were all one member, where were the body? But now are they many members, yet but one body...That there should be no schism in the body; but that the members should have the same care one for another. And whether one member suffer, all the members suffer with it; or one member be honored, all the members rejoice with it. Now ye are the body of Christ, and members in particular"* (1 Cor. 12:18, 19, 20, 25-27).

Prayer: Lord, I thank you for the local church. Help me to find my place in your body and to give faithful service there. I know that I need my fellow-believers. May I never forsake the assembling together of your local body.[1]

Pour your grace upon this local church. Give us a spirit of wisdom and revelation that we may know you better each day than the day before.[2] Strengthen us with power by your Spirit and fill us with all your fullness and grace.[3] So work in us that the fruit of your Spirit is experienced in purity and godliness.[4] Help us to see that we are one body in you, Lord, and to preserve the unity of the Spirit in the bond of peace.[5] Teach us to rejoice with each other, to suffer with each other and to accept and encourage each other. Knit our hearts together in love.[6]

Empower us by the Holy Spirit to be witnesses for you.[7] Grant us to speak your Word with all boldness.[8] Let your Word have free course,[9] grow mightily and prevail throughout this community.[10]

Lord, you said that the gates of hell would not prevail against your Church.[11] therefore, I ask that all the influence of the powers of darkness in this community be broken and destroyed. Let your Holy Spirit move in such power that multitudes are saved and every knee bow and every tongue confess that Jesus Christ is Lord.[12]

Father, make your grace abound toward your people. Give them good paying, stable jobs. Bless them with a willingness and ability to give their tithes and offerings with a generous and cheerful heart.[13]

Lord Jesus, we love you because you first loved us.[14] Help every one of us to truly love one another as you have loved us. In this way all men will know that we are your disciples.[15]

O, that people would learn to praise you for your goodness, Lord, and for your wonderful works to the children of men.[16] Let people come to your sanctuary to exalt you and praise you. Let us share your life as we worship you.

References: (1)Hebrews 10:25 (2)Ephesians 1:17
(3)Ephesians 3:16,19 (4)Galatians 5:22 (5)Ephesians 4:3,4
(6)Colossians 2:2 (7)Acts 1:8 (8)Acts 4:29 (9)2 Thessalonians 3:1
(10)Acts 19:20 (11)Matthew 16:18 (12)Philippians 2:10,11
(13)2 Corinthians 9:6-10 (14)1 John 4:19 (15)John 13:34,35
(16)Psalms 107:8.

100
Local Church Leaders

Key Thought: Those in leadership are gifts from God.

Key Scripture: *"And he gave some, apostles; and some, prophets; and some, evangelists; and some, pastors and teachers; For the perfecting of the saints, for the work of the ministry, for the edifying of the body of Christ: Till we all come in the unity of the faith, and of the knowledge of the Son of God, unto a perfect man, unto the measure of the stature of the fullness of Christ"* *(Eph. 4:11-13).*

Prayer: Lord, I thank you for our pastor(s), elders and other church leaders whom you have placed in the local body to keep us from being tossed to and fro, and carried about with every wind of doctrine, by the sleight of men, and cunning craftiness. Speaking the truth in love, let us grow up into you, Lord, in all things, for you are the head of the body.[1]

Bless our leaders, Lord, that they might govern your church according to your will. Help them be shepherds who never scatter the sheep,[2] but who care for the flock,[3] who watch for their souls,[4] and seek those who are lost and troubled.[5] Help me to be a support to them, to be available when they need me, to be always willing to help them and to pray for them.

As Aaron and Hur upheld the arms of Moses in the heat of the battle, so may we ever uphold the arms of those you have appointed to lead us.[6]

Fill our leaders with the knowledge of your will in all wisdom and spiritual understanding. Let them walk worthy of you, Lord, pleasing you by being fruitful in every good work, and increasing in the knowledge of you daily.

Let them be strengthened with all might according to all patience and longsuffering (endurance) with joyfulness.[7]

Multiply your grace and peace unto them through the knowledge of God and of Jesus, our Lord.[8] May they be esteemed by you because they have humble and contrite hearts and tremble at your Word.[9]

Release your righteousness, peace and joy into their lives.[10] Let your kingdom come and your will be done in them as it is in heaven.[11] Bless them and fill them with your Spirit, Lord.[12] Lead them in the way of escape from every temptation.[13] Keep their lives holy [14] and pure [15] before you. Protect them and their loved ones from the evil one.[16]

Prosper them and give them health, Lord.[17] Bless them financially. Give them helpers who are full of the Spirit and wisdom to whom they can delegate needed duties, so that they can give themselves to prayer and the ministry of the Word.[18]

Grant them the joy of having every member of their families saved and healthy. Bless their family life with special love and harmony.

Lord, I pray that they always remember you, their first love.[19] May they nurture that love relationship and grow closer and closer to you.[20]

References: (1)*Ephesians 4:14,15* (2)*Jeremiah 23:1* (3)*Jeremiah 23:4* (4)*Hebrews 13:17* (5)*Matthew 18:11-14* (6)*Exodus 17:10-13* (7)*Colossians 1:9-13* (8)*2 Peter 1:2* (9)*Isaiah 66:2* (10)*Romans 14:17* (11)*Matthew 6:10* (12)*Ephesians 5:18* (13)*1 Corinthians 10:13* (14)*1 Peter 1:16* (15)*1 John 3:3* (16)*Matthew 6:13* (17)*3 John 2* (18)*Acts 6:3,4* (19)*Revelation 2:4* (20)*James 4:8.* *Other Scriptures:* *Ezekiel 34:1-23, Romans 12:7, 2 Corinthians 4:1, 2 Corinthians 5:18.*

101
Revival in the Church

Key Thought: All revival stems from prayer.

Key Scripture: *"Wilt thou not revive us again: that thy people may rejoice in thee? Shew us thy mercy, O Lord, and grant us thy salvation"* (Ps. 85:6,7).

Prayer: Lord Jesus, thank you for your Church, the fellowship of the redeemed, the family of God, the called out ones. Keep us from the sin of indifference, the kind of lukewarmness that prevents your people from being either cold or hot. Your Word declares that you judge a church that is lukewarm.[1] Send revival to your Church, Lord, so that we are ablaze with your love and glory.

Pour out your abundant grace upon the Church, that your people will repent, turn to you, seek your face and respond to your call.

Comfort the hearts of your people. Knit us together in love, and unto all riches of the full assurance of understanding, to the acknowledgement of the mystery of God, and of you, Father, and of Christ in whom are hidden all the treasures of wisdom and knowledge.[2]

Help us, as your people, to see ourselves as you intended us to be — the light of the world — and to remember that a city that is set on a hill cannot be hid.[3] Help your Church to become that city, Lord; the city of God to which people will come to be redeemed. Let multitudes come and be saved.

Help me to remember that the key to revival is found in prayer. I will put on the whole armour of God and will pray always with all prayer and supplication in the Spirit and watch with all perseverance and supplication for all saints.[4] Though I walk in the midst of trouble, you will revive me. You will stretch forth your hand against the wrath of my enemies, and your right hand will save me. You will perfect that which concerns me. Your mercy, O Lord, endures forever. Forsake not the work of your hands.[5] Let your revival begin in me.

You dwell in the high and holy place, with all who are of a humble and contrite spirit, and you revive the spirit of the humble. You revive the hearts of all who are contrite. Help me to be broken, humble and contrite before you and others, Lord.[6] You have promised to bring revival to all who humble themselves and seek your face through prayer.[7] Give me, and all your people, a renewed spirit of prayer and humility.

Lord Jesus, grant that your Church would be rooted and grounded in you. Establish us in faith as we have been taught. Let us abound in thanksgiving.[8]

Thank you for the wonderful promise of your Word that they who wait upon you shall renew their strength. We will mount up with wings as eagles. We will run and not be weary. We will walk and not faint because you are giving revival to us.[9]

O Lord, revive your work in the midst of the years. Make your will known to your Church.[10] Send revival to your people till the glory of the Lord shall cover the earth as the waters cover the seas.[11]

References: (1)Revelation 3:15,16 (2)Colossians 2:2,3 (3)Matthew 5:14 (4)Ephesians 6:11,18 (5)Psalms 138:7,8 (6)Isaiah 57:15 (7)2 Chronicles 7:14 (8)Colossians 2:7 (9)Isaiah 40:31 (10)Habakkuk 3:2 (11)Habakkuk 2:14

PRAYERS THAT PREVAIL

PART V
Prayers for the Family

A. For Parents and Children

B. For Husbands and Wives

FOR PARENTS AND CHILDREN

102

When Someone Desires a Child

Key Thought: God hears your prayers.

Key Scripture: *"Now unto him that is able to do exceeding abundantly above all that we ask or think, according to the power that worketh in us, Unto him be glory in the church by Christ Jesus throughout all ages, world without end. Amen"* (Eph. 3:20, 21).

Prayer: Thank you for children, Father. They make life sweet and challenging. Praise you, Lord! You love to bless your people. I'm asking you now to bless _____ _____ with the baby he/she/they so desire(s), for children are an heritage from you and the fruit of the womb is a reward.[1]

You make the barren woman to be a joyful mother as you did in the case of Sara.[2] It was through faith that Sara received strength to conceive seed, and she was delivered of a child when she was past age because she trusted in your faithfulness,[3] Lord.

Impart faith and hope to the heart of _____ _____ so that he/she/they will not grow discouraged. Show him/her/them your will.

Help _____ to keep on believing and to trust you in this matter of his/her/their desire to have a baby. Protect his/her/their heart(s) and mind(s) that he/she/they will not to be confounded[4] or disheartened by negative words of others.

As arrows are in the hand of a mighty man, so are children of the youth. Happy is the man that has his quiver full of them, and they shall not be ashamed for they will speak with the enemies in the gate.[5] I claim this promise from you, Lord, in behalf of _____.

Thank you for every prayer promise of your Word, Lord. You have assured us that whatsoever we ask we will receive from you if we keep your commandments and do those things that are pleasing in your sight.[6] Thank you, Father, for hearing my prayer in behalf of _____ _____, and for undertaking in behalf of him/her/them.

References: *(1)Psalms 127:3 (2)Psalms 113:9 (3)Hebrews 11:11 (4)Psalms 22:4,5 (5)Psalms 127:4,5 (6)1 John 3:22,23*
Other Scriptures: *Psalms 128:3,4, 1 Samuel 1:4,5,11,17,20, Ephesians 3:14-19*

103

The Home

Key Thought: God is the most essential element in any home.

Key Scripture: *"Choose you this day whom ye will serve; whether the gods which your fathers served that were on the other side of the flood, or the gods of the Amorites, in whose land ye dwell: but as for me and my house, we will serve the Lord" (Josh. 24:15).*

Prayer: Lord God, I thank you for the home that you have provided for me and my family. Bless our home, Lord, and keep it safe by night and day. Put your hedge of protection around our home;[1] let us dwell in safety. Thank you for blessing our home with all spiritual blessings in heavenly places in Christ.[2]

Help me to remember that my home is built through wisdom, and by understanding it will be established. By knowledge shall all the chambers of my home be filled with precious and pleasant riches.[3] Give me your wisdom, understanding and knowledge, Lord.

Your Word declares that the home of the righteous shall be filled with much treasure.[4] In times of wickedness, you have promised that the house of the righteous will stand.[5] Thank you, Father.

As for me and my house, we will serve you. I fear, revere and respect you, Lord, and I delight greatly in your commandments. Therefore, your promise is that my seed will be mighty upon earth and the generation of the upright will be blessed; that wealth and riches will be in my house and my righteousness in you will endure forever.[6] Thank you, Lord!

I believe on you, Lord Jesus Christ, and I know that you have saved me and will save my entire household.[7] Praise you, Lord, for your abundant blessings.

Teach us to pray together as a family under your Lordship. May we never forsake you. We put you first, Lord, and we choose to serve you all our days. Bless my spouse and my children and our extended family. Help me to take good care of all you've given to me.

References: (1)Job 1:10 (2)Ephesians 1:3 (3)Proverbs 24:3,4 (4)Proverbs 15:6 (5)Proverbs 12:7 (6)Psalms 112:1-3 (7)Acts 16:31

104
A Parent's Prayer

Key Thought: Parenting is a sacred privilege.

Key Scripture: *"Lo, children are an heritage of the Lord: and the fruit of the womb is his reward. As arrows are in the hand of a mighty man; so are children of the youth. Happy is the man that hath his quiver full of them"* (Ps. 127:3-5).

Prayer: Lord, thank you for my children. They are such a blessing and a rich treasure. Help me to value them in the same way you value them for of such is the kingdom of heaven.[1]

I commit myself to the important responsibility of training my children in the way they should go. Lord, I know that if I will do this faithfully, my children will not depart from my training and your guidance when they are older.[2]

Father, you are my Father and you show me how a parent should nurture and care for his children. Thank you for giving me your example and your Word to guide me as a parent in these difficult times.

Lord, let me be a loving parent who seeks to understand his/her child(ren). Let the emphasis of my relationship with my child(ren) be upon caring instead of controlling. Work through me, Lord, to reach my children. May I become my child(ren)'s "safe place," Lord, even as you are my refuge.

Teach me how to rule my home well, having my children in subjection with all gravity,[3] but never provoking them to anger or to wrath.[4] Help me to be fair with my children and to understand them even as you understand me. Turn my heart to my child(ren), and the heart(s) of my child(ren) to me,[5] that our home may be blessed and not cursed.

Thank you for giving such good gifts to us, your children, Lord. You have promised to give the Holy Spirit to all who ask you.[6] Pour out your Spirit upon my children in these days, Lord, that they may prophesy and see visions and bring glory to your name.[7]

Thank you for being my loving heavenly Father. Your love and your power enable me to be an effective parent, and I know this is your desire for me.

References: *(1)Luke 18:16 (2)Proverbs 22:6 (3)1 Timothy 3:4 (4)Ephesians 6:4 (5)Malachi 4:6 (6)Luke 11:13 (7)Joel 2:28* *Other Scriptures: Proverbs 17:6*

105
A Single Parent's Prayer

Key Thought: God's grace is sufficient for me.

Key Scripture: *"Our (my) help is in the name of the Lord, who made heaven and earth" (Ps. 124:8).*

Prayer: Lord God, you are so great, and greatly to be praised.[1] You will be my God forever.[2]

As I call upon you, I know you will deliver me. I will always glorify you.[3] Your promises are so beautiful to me.

Yes, I do at times feel lonely, Lord, but I know you hear my cry. You always attend to my prayer.[4] When my heart is overwhelmed, you lead me to the rock that is higher than I.[5]

Thank you, Father, for my child(ren). I realize he/she/they is/are a wonderful heritage you have given to me. I accept the fruit of the womb — my child(ren) — as a reward from your hands.[6]

You have promised, Lord, to be a parent to my child(ren) and to me.[7] Thank you for sharing the parental responsibilities with me and for showing me how to be an effective parent. You set the solitary in families.[8] Thank you for being a part of our family, Lord. You protect us, provide for us and watch out for us.

You, Lord, are my helper, and I will not fear what man shall do unto me.[9] Lord Jesus Christ, you are the same yesterday, today, and for ever.[10] I cast all my care on you, for you care for me.[11]

Instead of fretting and worrying, Lord, I want to learn to trust you with all my heart. Help me to be like Mary who chose what is better, knowing that it will not be taken away from me.[12]

I will take no thought for my life, what I shall eat, or what I shall drink; nor will I take thought for my body, what I will wear.[13] Neither shall I worry about my singleness for I have learned to be content (through your love and peace) in my present circumstances.[14] I know you will supply all our needs in your perfect way and your perfect timing.[15]

Thank you, Lord, for your promise to espouse me as your own.[16] I know that you will always be with me. I trust you to lead me in all the relationships of my life. I will wait upon you, Lord.[17]

Impart to me the wisdom and patience I need to parent my child(ren) properly, Lord. You give liberally to all who ask of you.[18] I express my faith to you now. I desire never to waver in my faith nor to be double-minded in any way. Wonderful Jesus, I want you to have the preeminence always in all that I say and do.[19] I trust in you with all my heart; and lean not to my own understanding. In all my ways I acknowledge you and you direct my paths.[20]

References: (1)Psalms 48:1 (2)Psalms 48:14 (3)Psalms 50:15
(4)Psalms 61:1,2 (5)Psalms 61:2 (6)Psalms 127:3 (7)Psalms 68:5

*(8)Psalms 68:6 (9)Hebrews 13:6 (10)Hebrews 13:8 (11)1 Peter 5:7
(12)Luke 10:42 (13)Matthew 6:25-34 (14)Philippians 4:11
(15)Philippians 4:19 (16)Jeremiah 31:32 (17)Psalms 27:14
(18)James 1:5 (19)Colossians 1:18 (20)Proverbs 3:5,6*

106
A Prayer for an Unborn Child

Key Thought: Each child is a precious gift of God's creation.

Key Scripture: *"For thou hast possessed my reins: thou hast covered me in my mother's womb. I will praise thee; for I am fearfully and wonderfully made: marvelous are thy works; and that my soul knoweth right well"* (Ps. 139:13,14).

Prayer: Thank you, Father, for the precious gift of life. To have the honor of welcoming this new baby into my/our home and family is a joyous privilege indeed. I praise you, Father, for this tiny person you are giving to me/us. He/she is fearfully and wonderfully made.[1]

Cover the womb with your love. Bless my/our child with a supernatural awareness of your presence. May he/she always know that you are with him/her. May he/she always be sensitive to your Spirit. As he/she learns to bond together with us/me, his/her parent(s), may he/she also learn to bond with you.

I thank you, Father, that you see my/our baby's substance even as he/she is being made in secret.[2] You know him/her intimately. Begin even now, Lord, to call him/her and to prepare his/her heart to respond to you.[3]

Grant good health and vitality to my/our precious baby. As you take him/her from the womb, make him/her hope in you.[4] May he/she be cast upon you from the womb.[5] Be his/her God from now throughout eternity.

Strengthen this child even now, Lord. May he/she trust you with all his/her heart.[6] Guide him/her from the womb. Fashion him/her according to your purposes.[7] Form him/her from the womb to be your servant, Father.[8]

Even as John the Baptist leaped for joy within the womb of Elisabeth, his mother, when he became aware of your presence, may my/our baby develop a spiritual sensitivity that will lead him/her to recognize your presence and your voice.[9]

Lord Jesus, I thank you for your great love for children.[10] May my/our child know your love and acceptance throughout his/her life, and may he/she always trust and love you.

Blessed be the God and Father of my Lord Jesus Christ, who hath blessed us with all spiritual blessings in heavenly places in Christ. According as you, Lord, have chosen us before the foundation of the world, so choose my/our precious unborn child to be holy and without blame before you in love.[11]

May I ever be like your handmaiden Hannah who prayed, "For this child I prayed; and the Lord hath given me my petition which I asked of him. Therefore also I have lent him to the Lord; as long as he liveth he shall be lent to the Lord."[12]

Lord, I present my/our baby to you. Bless him/her. Lead him/her throughout his/her life. Thank you for blessing me/us with him/her. Use this child to bring glory to your name.

My heart rejoices in your goodness. I bask in your blessing and in your salvation.[13] I dedicate the life and future of this unborn child to you and your service.

References: (1)*Psalms 139:14* (2)*Psalms 139:15* (3)*Isaiah 49:1* (4)*Psalms 22:9* (5)*Psalms 22:10* (6)*Psalms 71:6* (7)*Job 31:15* (8)*Isaiah 49:5* (9)*Luke 1:41* (10)*Matthew 19:14* (11)*Ephesians 1:4* (12)*1 Samuel 1:28* (13)*1 Samuel 2:1*

FOR HUSBANDS AND WIVES

107

A Husband's Prayer

Key Thought: Marriage is a divine institution.

Key Scripture: *"Husbands, love your wives, even as Christ also loved the church, and gave himself for it" (Eph. 5:25).*

Prayer: Lord Jesus Christ, thank you for loving your Church and giving yourself for it. Thank you for the precious wife you have given to me and for all the blessings of a Christian marriage. Teach me how to love my wife as you love your bride, the Church.[1] Teach me how to give myself for my wife by providing for her, protecting her, helping her and understanding her.

Help me to love my wife always and never to grow bitter toward her.[2] Give me your grace to enable me to honor my wife, as the weaker vessel, so that we might be heirs together of the grace of life and so my prayers will not be hindered.[3]

Bless my marriage, Lord. May my wife and I live each for the other and both for you. Keep us together as we pray and work together. It is not good for a man to be alone,[4] and I praise you for giving me a wife who stands with me, supports me and respects me. She is my helpmeet in all I do. May I remember always to do those things that will help her respond to me in godly ways.

It is my desire, Lord, to rule my home well,[5] to teach my wife and children your precepts both through word and example,[6] and to endeavor to meet the needs of my family. Help me faithfully to bring up my children in the nurture and admonition of you[7] and to wash my wife with the water of your Word, even as you so wash your bride, the Church.[1] Thank you for the gift of marriage which is honorable in all and for the undefiled bed of marriage[8] where I can express my love for my wife.

I give you thanks always for all things in your name, Lord. Help my wife and me to submit ourselves to you and each other in reverential fear of you.[9]

It is a privilege for me to be a husband, Lord. Help me to be a faithful husband to the wife you have given to me.

References: (1)*Ephesians 5:25,26* (2)*Colossians 3:19* (3)*1 Peter 3:7* (4)*Genesis 2:18* (5)*1 Timothy 3:12* (6)*Deuteronomy 6:6,7* (7)*Ephesians 6:4* (8)*Hebrews 13:4* (9)*Ephesians 5:20,21*
Other Scriptures: *Luke 16:18, 1 Corinthians 7*

108
A Wife's Prayer

Key Thought: The worth of a virtuous woman is immeasurable.

Key Scripture: *"Who can find a virtuous woman? for her price is far above rubies. The heart of her husband doth safely trust in her, so that he shall have no need of spoil. She will do him good and not evil all the days of her life"* (Prov. 31:10-12).

Prayer: Heavenly Father, I thank you for my husband. Help me to see my role as his wife as a sacred calling. Continue your workmanship in my life so that my husband's heart will safely trust in me. May I do him good and not evil all the days of my life.

Through your grace, I will submit myself unto my husband, as unto you. Help me to see my husband as my head in the same way as you are the Head of your Church. As the Church is subject to you, let me be subject to my husband in everything.[1]

Let me reverence my husband[2] and help me to feel secure in his love for me. I ask this in your name, Lord Jesus, giving thanks for the husband you have provided for me. I submit to my husband heartily, as to you, Lord, knowing that I shall receive the reward of the inheritance.[3]

Help me always to look well to the ways of my household, to be faithful to my responsibilities as my husband's helpmeet. Teach me to honor the role of wife and mother, even though the world seems increasingly to despise it. Give me wisdom, help me be industrious, let the law of kindness be in my tongue, that my husband and children may truly call me blessed.[4]

May I learn to render unto my husband his due benevolence and may I never defraud the man you have given to me in any way.[5] I desire to reverence my husband and give him honor all the days of my life.[6]

Teach me to be reverent, temperate (self-controlled) and faithful in all things.[7] Help me to remember that my behavior will enable me to win my husband to you when he does not obey your Word.[8] Adorn my life, Lord, with a meek and quiet spirit which is of great price in your sight.[9] Teach me to trust you, Lord, to work in my husband's life in the best possible way.

I commit myself to doing all that is possible to preserve our unity as husband and wife, so that together we will be heirs of the grace of life and our prayers will not be hindered.[10]

References: *(1)Ephesians 5:22-24 (2)Ephesians 5:33*
(3)Colossians 3:23,24 (4)Proverbs 31 (5)1 Corinthians 7:3-5
(6)Esther 1:20 (7)1 Timothy 3:11 AMP (8)1 Peter 3:1
(9)1 Peter 3:4 (10)1 Peter 3:7 **Other Scriptures:** *1 Corinthians 7*

PRAYERS THAT PREVAIL

Prayer Journal

ALSO AVAILABLE

☆ ☆ ☆ ☆ ☆ ☆

PRAYERS THAT PREVAIL FOR AMERICA–Changing a Nation
Through Prayer: An Intercessor's Manual by the authors of the best-
selling *Prayers That Prevail.* Learn how to pray God's powerful promises
in behalf of our nation, our leaders, our people and our problems. Take
America back through sixty topical prayers from the Bible that invoke
God's blessings and mercy for our land. In addition to the prayers, this
dynamic book includes "A Call to Intercession," a look at "The
Presidents and Prayer," "One Nation Under God," and "Fifty Prayer
Promises." For every Christian who is concerned about America.

Date   Notes and Comments

Date   Notes and Comments

Date   Notes and Comments

Date	Notes and Comments

Date   Notes and Comments

Date	Notes and Comments

Date   Notes and Comments

Prayer Journal

Date

Notes and Comments

Date   Notes and Comments

Date	Notes and Comments

Date	Notes and Comments

Date	Notes and Comments

Date	Notes and Comments

Prayer Journal

Date	Notes and Comments

Date   Notes and Comments

Date   Notes and Comments

Date   Notes and Comments

Date	Notes and Comments

Date

Notes and Comments

Date   Notes and Comments

Date   Notes and Comments

Date	Notes and Comments

Date   Notes and Comments

Date	Notes and Comments

Date	Notes and Comments

Date	Notes and Comments

Date   Notes and Comments

Date	Notes and Comments

Date   Notes and Comments

Date   Notes and Comments